Chef Wan **Around the World**

TIMES EDITIONS

The Publisher wishes to thank **METROJAYA BERHAD**, Malaysia for the loan of their crockery and utensils.

Food Preparation: **Chef Norzailina Nordin**
Project Editor/Editor of the Malay Edition: **Jamilah Mohd Hassan**
Art Direction/Designer: **Christopher Wong**
Photographer: **Jenhor Siow**
Editor of the English Edition: **Lydia Leong**
Project Co-ordinator: **Christine Chong**
Production Co-ordinator: **Nor Sidah Haron**

Published by Times Editions
An imprint of Times Media Private Limited
A member of the Times Publishing Group

Times Centre, 1 New Industrial Road, Singapore 536196
Tel: (65) 6213 9288   Fax: (65) 6285 4871
E-mail: te@tpl.com.sg
Online Book Store: http://www.timesone.com.sg/te

Times Subang, Lot 46 Subang Hi-Tech Industrial Park
Batu Tiga, 40000 Shah Alam, Selangor Darul Ehsan, Malaysia
Tel & Fax: (603) 5636 3517   E-mail: cchong@tpg.com.my

National Library Board (Singapore) Cataloguing in Publication Data

Wan, Chef, 1958-
Chef Wan : Around the world – Singapore : Times Editions, 2003.
p. cm.

ISBN : 9812322043

1. Cookery, International. I. Title.

TX725.A1
641.59— dc21
SLS2002044720

Printed by Times Printers Pte Ltd

A food critic and writer for various magazines in Malaysia, Chef Wan also makes regular appearances on Malaysian television. He has hosted various cooking programmes in Singapore, Australia, Norway and the United States, and co-hosted culinary tour shows with another celebrity chef, Martin Yan in Malaysia, Singapore and the Philippines. He has also appeared as a guest chef in South Africa and London's BBC.

The well-travelled chef has worked in various countries including the United States, Canada, Italy, France and Hong Kong, and onboard the cruise liner, *Royal Viking*. As the resident chef of a Hawaiian patron, Chef Wan cooked for visiting celebrities.

Chef Wan holds an Associate Degree in professional Chef Training and Hotel Management from the California Culinary Academy, San Francisco, and a degree from Ritz Hotel's Ritz Escoffier Ecole de Gastonomie FranÁaise, Paris. Today he is a visiting chef to the Ritz Escoffier Ecole de Gastonomie FranÁaise, Paris, the Cipriani Cooking School in Venice and other culinary academies in London, Australia and Singapore.

Asian

Middleeastern

Mediterranean

European

Caribbean

American

asian

The Philippines ✤ Sri Lanka ✤ Vietnam ✤ Thailand ✤ Indonesia

Escabeche
(Pickled Fried Fish)

A dish of Spanish origin, Escabeche is either poached or fried. In this recipe, the fish is fried, resulting in a light and crisp skin that seals in the juices while providing an excellent contrast to the tangy sauce.

Ingredients:

Threadfin	1 medium

Marinade:

Salt	1 tsp
Fresh lemon juice	exctracted from 1 lemon

Sauce:

Cooking oil for deep-frying	
Garlic	2 cloves, peeled and finely chopped
Shallots	2, peeled and finely sliced
Ginger	1-cm knob, peeled and cut into strips
Onion	1 medium, peeled and cut into thin rings
Carrot	1 small, peeled and cut into strips
White vinegar	1/4 cup
Water	1/4 cup
Sugar	55 g
Salt	1/2 tsp
Dark soy sauce	1/2 Tbsp
Light soy sauce	2 Tbsp
Corn flour (cornstarch)	1 tsp, dissolved in 2 Tbsp water

Method

- Season the fish with salt and lemon juice. Set aside to marinate for 20 minutes.
- Heat the cooking oil in a pan over moderate heat until hot.
- Remove the fish from marinade. Fry in hot oil until golden brown on both sides. Transfer the fish to a paper-lined dish to drain.
- Leave 1 Tbsp cooking oil in the pan and discard the rest. Sauté the garlic, shallots and ginger for 2 minutes. Add onion and carrot and stir-fry for another 2 minutes. Pour in the vinegar, water, sugar, salt, dark and light soy sauce. Bring to boil and stir in the corn flour solution. Simmer until the sauce thickens.
- Transfer the fish to a serving dish. Pour the sauce over the fish and serve hot.

Chicken Adobo with Pineapple

This is another dish of Spanish influence. In Mexico, Adobo refers to a marinade of various spices, herbs and vinegar. The Filipinos modified the recipe, adding soy sauce and ground pepper. Chicken Abodo is one of the best-known Filipino dishes.

Ingredients:

Cooking oil for deep-frying	
Chicken	1.5 kg, parts or whole, cut into small pieces

Marinade:

Salt	1/2 tsp
Ground white pepper	1/2 tsp

Sauce:

Shallots	2, peeled and sliced
Garlic	4 cloves, peeled and chopped
Bay leaf	1
Chicken stock granules	2 Tbsp
Light soy sauce	2 Tbsp
White vinegar	1/2 cup
Water	1/2 cup
Fresh pineapple	400 g, cubed
Tomatoes	2 medium, quartered

Garnishing:

Spring onions (scallion)	2, cut into 5-cm lengths
Red capsicum (bell pepper)	1, cut into thin strips

Method:

- Heat the cooking oil in a pan over moderate heat.
- Pat the chicken pieces dry. Season with salt and pepper. Fry until golden brown. Transfer chicken to a paper-lined dish to drain.
- Leave 1 Tbsp cooking oil in the pan and discard the rest. Fry the shallots and garlic until crisp. Add the chicken, bay leaf, chicken stock granules, soy sauce, vinegar and water. Cover the pan and simmer for 25 minutes. Add the pineapple cubes and tomato quarters and stir for 2 minutes.
- Transfer to a serving dish, garnish with spring onions and capsicums and serve.

Malu Bola Cutlis
(Spanish Mackerel Balls)

The mashed potato holds the ingredients together and adds substance to the dish. It also makes these Spanish mackerel balls a complete meal on their own. Serve them as part of main meal or a midday snack.

Ingredients:

Mackerel Balls:

Spanish mackerel	400 g, steamed, deboned and minced (ground)
Potatoes	500g, peeled, boiled and mashed
Onion	1, peeled, sliced and fried
Egg	1, beaten
Bread	2 slices, soaked in fresh milk and drained
Fish curry powder	1¹/₂ tsp
Dried dill	1 tsp
Salt	¹/₄ tsp
Ground white pepper	¹/₄ tsp

Coating:

Plain (all-purpose) flour	150 g
Egg	1, beaten
Breadcrumbs	100 grams

Cooking oil for deep-frying

wan-derings

DESPITE its small geographical size, Sri Lanka has a diverse and rich heritage of authentic cooking styles. I visited the republic to attend a Sri Lankan wedding ceremony several years ago and had the opportunity to watch the womenfolk preparing the celebratory meal. As they worked, they were also chatting and chewing betel nuts. They were preparing a dish of mackerel cutlets and the smell of dill and curry spices was heavenly! Experience it for yourself with this recipe!

I believe the use of dill (often used in Western-style cooking especially for seafood dishes) has Portuguese roots. It was brought into Sri Lankan cooking when the Portuguese colonised Sri Lanka in the 16th century. If you can't locate the herb, you may substitute it with coriander leaves (cilantro).

Method:
- Combine all the ingredients for Mackerel Balls and mix well into a paste. Shape the mixture into small balls.
- Dust the balls in flour. Dip in beaten egg and coat with breadcrumbs.
- Heat the cooking oil in a pan over moderate heat until hot. Fry the mackerel balls until golden brown. Drain and serve.

Prawn Jingka

This lovely dish is usually served with paratha or naan. You may also use it as a sandwich filling. As a variation to the recipe, you may replace the prawns (shrimps) with fish or crabmeat. Whichever meat you choose to use, the taste is truly sensational!

Ingredients:

Ghee	1 Tbsp
Onion	1, peeled and cut into cubes
Garlic	3 cloves, peeled and finely chopped
Chilli powder	2 Tbsp
Ground turmeric	1 tsp
Ground cloves	1/4 tsp
Ground cinnamon	1/4 tsp
Coconut milk	1 cup
King prawns (jumbo shrimps)	1 kg, feelers and legs trimmed, and deveined
Salt and sugar to taste	
Tomatoes	2, sliced
Lime juice	extracted from 1/2 lime
Coriander leaves (cilantro)	1 Tbsp, chopped

Method:

- Heat the ghee in a pan over moderate heat. Sauté the onion and garlic until golden brown. Add the chilli powder and ground turmeric.
- Turn the heat to low and continue frying. Add the ground cloves, cinnamon and coconut milk. Stir well and simmer until the gravy is reduced to half its original volume.
- Add the prawns, salt, sugar and tomatoes. Simmer until the gravy thickens slightly.
- Transfer to a serving dish. Drizzle with lime juice, garnish with coriander leaves and serve.

Vietnamese Fried Prawns

This deliciously spicy dish can be prepared in a few quick and easy steps. For a less spicy dish, remove the seeds from the chillies before grinding. Wear gloves when handling chillies to avoid the burning sensation they may leave on your hands. This dish goes well with rice.

Ingredients:

Large prawns (shrimps)	1 kg, feelers and legs trimmed and deveined

Marinade:

Light soy sauce	2 Tbsp
Garlic	3 cloves, peeled and finely minced
Ground white pepper	1 tsp
Lemon grass	2 stalks, sliced and finely ground

Sauce:

Cooking oil	1 Tbsp
Lemon grass	4 stalks, thinly sliced
Red chillies	8, finely ground
Dried shrimp paste	1 tsp, roasted and finely ground
Mint leaves	1 handful
Lime juice	1 lime
Anchovy stock granules	1 tsp
Fish sauce (*nuoc nam*)	2 Tbsp
Roasted groundnuts	3 Tbsp, coarsely pounded
Sugar to taste	

Method:

- Put prawns in marinade and leave for 1 hour.
- Heat the cooking oil in a pan over moderate heat until hot. Sauté the lemon grass slices. Add the chillies, shrimp paste, mint leaves, lime juice, anchovy stock granules, fish sauce, groundnuts and sugar to taste. Stir well.
- Add the prawns and sauté till prawns are just cooked. Remove from heat and serve hot.

w a n - derings

THERE is a certain refinement and quality in Vietnamese cuisine that distinguishes it from the cuisines of other Asian countries. Although influenced by the cuisines of China, France and India, Vietnamese cuisine retains an authentic flavour, with its unique use of herbs. While this may sound complex, the techniques of preparing Vietnamese cuisine are, however, rather simple.

In the south, you will find that the food is spicier compared to that of the north. Southern Vietnam produces a hot chilli powder and a variety of herbs, which they use freely in their cooking. Lemon grass, coriander, garlic, Chinese chives, basil (*rau que*) or Thai basil, g*iap ca, ngo gai* and *ngo om* are generously used in salads and noodles. What makes Vietnamese food special is certainly the mixture and use of these basic ingredients. The long coastline of Vietnam also means that there is an abundant supply of seafood, which is reflected in their choice of meats when cooking.

The Vietnamese use chopsticks and metal spoons, and small saucers of condiments such as *nuoc cham*, a clear salty fish sauce, accompany every meal. Other than *nuoc cham*, there is *nuoc mam*. The latter is spicier and saltier. Although it is also rather pungent, the smell disappears when mixed with food.

Desserts served in the Vietnamese home consist mostly of fresh fruits, while cakes and coffees are found in cafes in cities and towns. In between meals, the Vietnamese favour French-styled sandwiches and pint-size savoury snacks.

Kaeng Phet Kai Sai No Mai
(Thai Chicken Curry)

This dish can be rather spicy, depending on the chillies used. For a milder dish, remove the seeds from the chillies before grinding. This dish goes very well with white rice.

Ingredients:

List A:

Shallots	10, peeled
Garlic	4 cloves, peeled
Lemon grass	4 stalks
Coriander (cilantro) roots	6
Galangal	1-cm knob, peeled
Coriander seeds	1 Tbsp
Ground black pepper	2 tsp
Kaffir lime rind	grated from 1 kaffir lime
Kaffir lime leaves	2
Dried chillies	15–20
Shrimp paste	2 tsp, crushed

List B:

Cooking oil	¼ cup
Chicken	1 kg, cut into 8–10 pieces
Coconut milk	4 cups, extracted from 400 g grated coconut and 4 cups water
Pickled bamboo shoots	200 g
Kaffir lime leaves	3
Fish sauce (*nam pla*)	2 Tbsp
Salt and sugar to taste	
Thai basils (*bai horapa*)	½ cup, chopped

Method:

- Blend the ingredients in List A into a finely ground paste.
- Heat the cooking oil and sauté the finely ground paste until fragrant. Stir in the chicken and coconut milk. Simmer over low heat for 20 minutes.
- When the chicken is tender, add the bamboo shoots, kaffir lime leaves, fish sauce, salt, sugar and basil leaves. Cook for another 10 minutes, remove from heat and serve.

Wan-derings

IN recent years, Thai cuisine has gained popularity as an exotic food worldwide. No other Asian cuisine shares the same amount of popularity. I believe it is the Thai people's creative use of spices that has made Thai cuisine so popular and so unique.

Thai food is light and refreshing. It is also varied, ranging from the hot and spicy to the mild. The secret of Thai cooking is to create a balanced flavour with the use of spices to enhance the taste of the dish.

The most popular desserts in Thailand are fruits, but on special occasions, *takaw,* tapioca flour confections and a variety of sugar and coconut desserts are served.

Ayam Panggang Bumbu Rojak
(Spicy Grilled Chicken)

This recipe was given to me by Mdm Sudarmaji, the wife of the Indonesian Ambassador to Malaysia, in 1994. This dish has its origins in the golden era of Java and it is still served at feasts in central Java today. I would recommend using *kampung* (or free range) chicken, if possible, as it would help make the dish tastier.

Ingredients:

Chicken	1 (3 kg)
Coconut milk	2 cups
Salt and sugar to taste	

List A:

Red chillies	8
Fresh turmeric	1-cm knob, peeled
Garlic	4 cloves, peeled
Lemon grass	3 stalks, finely sliced
Ground coriander	1 tsp
Ginger	½-cm knob, peeled
Galangal	½-cm knob, peeled
Shallots	10, peeled
Candlenuts	6

Method:
- Blend the ingredients in List A in a food processor to achieve a smooth paste.
- In a pan, add in the paste, chicken, coconut milk, salt and sugar and boil for 20 minutes over medium heat. Remove the chicken and continue boiling the sauce until it begins to thicken. Remove from heat.
- Grill (broil) the chicken on a charcoal grill, turning it over periodically and basting with the sauce. Grill until the chicken is cooked. Test using a skewer. The juices should run clear. Serve hot.

wan-derings

INDONESIA is the world's largest archipelago and its terrain is a mix of coastal lowlands and interior mountains. It is one of the most populated countries in the world, made up of people of diverse ethnicities. Its geographical and cultural mix have contributed towards the country's wide variety of cooking styles and dishes. However, its cuisine is little-known abroad.

In general, Indonesian cuisine is very aromatic and favours the use of hot chilli paste, coconut milk, lemon grass, herbs and dark soy sauce. Some of the most well known dishes include hot curry, pickled fish and spicy saté. Javanese cooking uses less chillies but is also rich and flavourful. Coconut milk and brown sugar are common ingredients.

In Bali, the dishes are simple yet interesting and are always served with care. Rice is usually served with leafy green vegetables in coconut milk gravy. Fruits and vegetables are also flavoured with tasty sauces. These include fruit *rojak* (fruit salad) and *gado-gado* (vegetable salad with rice cake), which are cooked using sweet soy sauce, light soy sauce and chilli.

Rijsttafel is the most elaborate of all Indonesia's dishes. Its royal name originated from the era of the flourishing spice trade. It refers to a meal consisting of a wide selection of dishes including curries, meat, seafood, porridge, eggs, and salads. Guests are seated at beautifully decorated long tables and are served by waiters dressed in batik. Today, this meal is served at restaurants throughout the world, although the selection of dishes may be reduced. At smaller restaurants, Rijsttafel may be served buffet-style.

In Indonesia, food enhancers and side dishes are as important as main dishes. Among them are fried tempe, bean curd, anchovies, pickle and nuts, *keropok* (fish or prawn/shrimp crackers), *serunding* (roasted grated coconut with peanuts) and *rempeyek kacang* (savoury groundnut brittle).

Kalasan Fried Chicken

A popular dish from Central Java, this aromatic chicken meal is best served with rice and a sweet soy sauce for dipping. Boiling the chicken first ensures that the meat remains tender even after it is fried.

Ingredients:

Cooking oil for frying	
Coconut milk	4 cups, extracted from 400g white grated coconut and 4 cups water
Chicken	1 (2–3 kg), cut into 2 pieces
Kaffir lime leaves	2
Salt and pepper to taste	
Shallots, crisp-fried for garnishing	
Coriander leaves (cilantro) for garnishing	

List A:

Kaffir lime leaves	2
Lemon grass	3 stalks, sliced
Fresh turmeric	1-cm knob, peeled
Galangal	1-cm knob, peeled
Onions	2, peeled and cut into cubes
Red chillies	6

Method:

- Blend the ingredients in List A in a food processor to achieve a smooth paste.
- Heat 3 Tbsp of cooking oil and stir-fry the paste until fragrant. Add coconut milk and stir well.
- Add chicken and kaffir lime leaves. Cook for 25 minutes until chicken is tender. Remove chicken from the sauce.
- Leave the sauce to simmer until it thickens. Season with salt and pepper.
- Deep-fry the chicken until golden brown. Drain and place on a serving dish. Pour the sauce over, garnish with crisp-fried shallots and coriander leaves (cilantro) before serving.

middle eastern

Avocado Catalan Salad

This colourful salad recipe from my friend Chef Joyce Goldstein is one of my favourite. I have simply added white pepper for a bit of spice. Each time I serve this salad for dinner, everyone raves about the dressing. You do not need to soak the almonds to remove the skin, as it tastes good with the skin on. Just bake the almonds in the oven at 180°C for about 5 minutes or until it turns brown.

Ingredients:

Salad Dressing:

Olive oil	1 cup
Sherry vinegar	1/4 cup
Lime juice	1/4 cup
Sliced almonds	75 g
Capers	2 Tbsp, finely chopped
Lime rind	2 Tbsp, grated
Anchovies	2 Tbsp, pounded to a paste
Salt and ground white pepper to taste	

Salad:

Avocadoes	2 almost ripe, stoned, peeled and sliced
Oranges	2, peeled and sliced
Red capsicum (bell pepper)	1, sliced, grilled (broiled) and peeled
Lettuce leaves as decoration	

wan-derings

MY KNOWLEDGE of Middle Eastern cooking began from dining in restaurants in Sydney and San Francisco, as well as reading and experimenting with recipes found in books. I also had the opportunity to work for several months in a small restaurant owned by a Lebanese in Vancouver, Canada.

I was inspired to learn about the cuisines of the Mediterranean and Middle Eastern countries by Joyce Goldstein, a famous chef and the owner of Square One, a very successful Mediterranean restaurant in San Francisco. Joyce was voted by the San Francisco FOCUS magazine as Chef of the Year in 1992. She also received the James Beard Perrier Jouet Award for Best Chef in California in 1993. She is the author of two cookbooks, *The Mediterranean* and *Back to Square One*. Although I have never worked with Joyce, my frequent visits to the restaurant resulted in us becoming good friends.

Method:

- Pour the ingredients for salad dressing into a food processor and blend for 1–2 minutes. Do not blend it too long as the almonds should not be too fine.
- Arrange the salad ingredients on a plate and pour the salad dressing over. Serve.

CHEF'S NOTE: You may garnish the salad with additional almond slices for added bite.

Patlican Boreg
(Fried Aubergine Sandwich)

This recipe originated from Turkey and is served as *mezzeh*. *Mezzeh* is a starter or appetiser and is usually served before the main meal. The word *mezzeh* comes from the Greek word *maza* which means "mixture". In Tunisia, *mezzeh* is known as *aadou* while in Algeria it is *kemia*.

In Middle Eastern cuisine, the most common *mezzeh* are meatballs, fish balls, stuffed quail, fried sardine kebabs, pickled vegetables and olives, cheese, nuts and fruits.

Ingredients:

Olive oil	½ cup
Aubergines (eggplants)	2, large and round, sliced into 1-cm thick slices
Salt and ground white pepper to taste	
Monterey Jack/Swiss cheese	250 g, grated
Eggs	3, beaten
Parsley leaves	3 Tbsp, chopped
Dill	1 tsp
Plain (all-purpose) flour	225 g, sifted
Breadcrumbs	200 g, from 2 slices of toasted bread, ground
Cooking oil for frying	

Method:

- Preheat the oven to 200°C.
- Grease the baking tray evenly with olive oil. Coat the aubergine slices with olive oil and arrange on a baking tray. Sprinkle salt and ground white pepper and bake for 15–20 minutes. Remove from oven.
- In a bowl, mix the cheese with half the portion of beaten eggs, parsley leaves and dill.
- Add a spoonful of the mixture on some of the aubergine slices and place the other slices on top to sandwich the mixture. Coat the aubergine sandwiches with flour. Dip in the remaining portion of beaten eggs and coat with bread-crumbs. Refrigerate for half hour before frying.
- Heat the cooking oil over low heat until hot. Dip the sandwiches in and fry until golden brown on both sides and the cheese is soft. Serve hot with tomato sauce.

CHEF'S NOTE: *This dish can be served as an accompaniment to barbecue lamb, barbecue chicken kebab or lamb chops.*

Baba Ghanoush

Aubergine (eggplant) puree is a popular *mezzeh*. In Lebanon, this puree is called Baba Ghanoush. There are various ways of preparing this dish. In Iran, dried fruits and yoghurt are added to the puree. According to Jemel, a Lebanese chef I met in Vancouver, the secret of this dish is to bring out the taste from the smoked aubergine. His technique is not to use glowing charcoal, which will burn the outer skin and to use lots of lemon juice. Besides serving this dish as a dip with pita bread, it is also lovely eaten as a sandwich spread with grilled (broiled) chicken.

Ingredients:

Aubergines (eggplants)	350 g
Garlic	3 cloves, peeled and pounded to a paste
Tahini (sesame seed paste)	2 Tbsp
Sour cream	4 Tbsp
Parsley leaves	1 Tbsp, chopped
Olive oil	2 Tbsp
A pinch of chilli powder	
Lemon juice	2 Tbsp
Salt to taste	

Method:

- Grill the aubergines until the skin darkens and the flesh is soft. Allow to cool. When cool, slice in two and scoop out the flesh.
- Put the aubergine flesh and the rest of the ingredients into the food processor and blend until smooth. Serve as a dip or use as a sandwich filling.

CHEF'S NOTE: *I have been to restaurants where the Baba Ghanoush served has a rather coarse texture. My preference is for the smoother version.*

Hummus Bi Tahina

This is probably the most famous *mezzeh* in the Middle East. I first tasted it when I attended a friend's party in Sydney, Australia, several years ago. He served it as a dip with pita bread and raw vegetables. It tasted so good, I finished the whole bowl! This hummus is made from chickpeas and a sesame seed paste known as *tahini*. Depending on your preference, you can regulate the food processor for a coarse or smooth textured dip.

Ingredients:

Chickpeas	1 can (225 g)
Tahini (sesame seed paste)	3 Tbsp
Garlic	3 cloves, peeled
Lemon juice	3 Tbsp
Olive oil	3 Tbsp
Salt and ground white pepper to taste	

Method:

- Combine all the ingredients and blend in a food processor. Regulate to make it as smooth or coarse as you prefer. Add some water if the mixture is too thick. Serve as a dip with cut vegetables or pita bread.

CHEF'S NOTE: *If you are unable to obtain tahini, use $1/4$ cup sesame seeds, fried until fragrant and pounded to a paste.*

Falafel

The Israelis consider Falafel their national food. It is popularly sold in roadside stalls in Jerusalem, Tel Aviv and Tiberias. In the Arabian countries, chickpeas are the main ingredient. I love making Falafel for afternoon tea. It is wonderful served as a finger food. Once you have tasted these Falafel, you will certainly be hooked!

Ingredients:

Chickpeas	500 g, soaked overnight in cold water
Baking soda	1 tsp
Garlic	3 cloves, peeled and finely chopped
Onion	1, peeled and finely chopped
Ground fennel	1 tsp
Ground coriander	1 tsp
Coriander leaves (cilantro)	1 Tbsp, finely chopped
A pinch of chilli powder	
Lemon juice	1 Tbsp
Tahini (sesame seed paste)	1 Tbsp
Breadcrumbs	100 g
Cooking oil for frying	

Method:

- Rinse the chickpeas thoroughly and blend in a food processor until it achieves a coarse texture. Add a little water if required.
- In a bowl, mix the blended chickpeas with the other ingredients and shape into balls using the palm of your hand. Coat the balls in breadcrumbs.
- Heat the cooking oil in a pan over moderate heat until hot. Turn the heat to low and fry the balls until golden brown. Drain and serve.

CHEF'S NOTE: *If you prefer a softer Falafel, you may substitute baking soda with 1/2 tsp instant yeast. If using yeast, mix the ingredients and set aside for half hour. Allow the dough to rise slightly before shaping and frying.*

Mahshi Filfil
(Stuffed Capsicums)

This dish of stuffed capsicums (bell peppers) can be found in almost all the Middle Eastern and Mediterranean countries. It should be eaten cold as an appetiser. A mixture of tamarind and sugar gives the dish a sweet and sour flavour. Although green capsicums are commonly used, a combination of red and yellow capsicums would add more colour. Besides capsicums, we can also use tomatoes, courgettes (zucchinis) () and onions.

Ingredients:

Capsicums (bell peppers)	6, medium
Olive oil	1/4 cup
Onion	1, peeled and finely chopped
Pine nuts	2 Tbsp
Currants	2 Tbsp
Salt and ground white pepper to taste	
Tamarind juice	1 1/2 Tbsp
Castor sugar	2 tsp
Water	2 5/8 cups, boiling hot
Fragrant rice	250 g
Parsley leaves	2 Tbsp, chopped
Mint leaves	2 Tbsp, finely chopped
Tomatoes	2, seeded and chopped
Spring onions (scallions)	5, finely sliced

Method:

- Preheat the oven to 190°C.
- Slice off the top of the capsicums and scoop out the flesh. Set aside.
- Heat a little olive oil and sauté the chopped onion until crisp and golden brown. Add pine nuts. Fry for a while before adding currants, salt and pepper. Add tamarind juice, castor sugar and boiling water. Pour in the rice.
- Add parsley and mint leaves, tomatoes, spring onions and cook over medium heat for about 10 minutes until the mixture is just slightly moist.
- Fill the capsicums with the mixture and replace with capsicum covers. Arrange filled capsicums neatly on a baking tray. Pour 5/8 cup water around the capsicums. Cover with aluminium foil and bake for 40 minutes. Remove aluminium foil and bake for another 20 minutes until the capsicums are tender.

Kefta

Several years ago, when I was living in Paris, I used to frequent a Lebanese restaurant, *Dar Lebanon*. I thoroughly enjoyed the Ghanouj kebab with pita bread, lamb kebab with pilaf rice, crunchy falafel and, of course, kefta. This recipe is a type of Lebanese kefta eaten stuffed in pita bread with salad leaves, cucumber and tomatoes.

Ingredients:

Beef or lamb	2 kg, washed and cut into pieces

Marinade:

Ground turmeric	1 tsp
Ground paprika	2 tsp
Chilli flakes	1 tsp
Parsley leaves	2 cups, chopped
Ground cinnamon	1¼ tsp
Salt and ground white pepper to taste	
Egg	1, lightly beaten

Method:

- Prepare the marinade and leave the meat to marinate for 2 hours in the refrigerator.
- Skewer the meat and grill (broil) over glowing charcoal until the meat is cooked.
- To serve, remove the meat from the skewer and place in pita bread. Serve with cucumber, lettuce leaves, tomatoes and sour yoghurt.

Lamb Couscous

Couscous is the culinary pride of the North African Berber and it is Morocco's national food. The couscous in Morocco is sweeter and less spicy compared to that served in Algeria and Tunisia. Traditionally, couscous was served before the main meal so that guests would not be able to eat much of the main course and the food would be brought back to the kitchen for the cooks!

The couscous sold in most major supermarket chains in Kuala Lumpur are usually half-cooked. It comes in boxes and needs to be soaked in salt water. Leave it to soak for about 10 minutes. Stir the couscous with your hands to ensure that the grains do not stick together. Steam uncovered in a steamer or couscousiere, a special set of pots used to steam couscous. Once steam is released from between the grains of couscous, it is ready. Mix with a little butter before serving.

Ingredients:

Butter	340 g
Onions	3, peeled and finely chopped
Beef or lamb	2 kg
Saffron strands	1 Tbsp
Ground black pepper	2 Tbsp
Ground turmeric	1 tsp
Water	8 cups
Carrots	3, peeled and cut into four pieces
Potatoes	2, peeled and cut into four pieces
Tomatoes	5, quartered
Aubergines (eggplants)	3, cut into four pieces
Courgettes (zucchinis	3, cut into four pieces
Couscous	1.6 kg, soaked and drained
Chickpeas	200 g, soaked overnight in water
Red chillies	2
Green chillies	3
Salt and ground black pepper to taste	
Coriander leaves as garnish	

Method:

- Melt 225 g butter in a pan over moderate heat. Add onions and sauté until soft. Add meat, saffron strands, black pepper and turmeric. Mix well.
- Pour the water, carrots and potatoes into the pan and bring to the boil. Leave to boil for half hour. Add other vegetables and cook for another 5 minutes. Add salt and pepper to taste. Remove from heat and set aside.
- Line a steamer with muslin or a thin cloth and fill with the prepared couscous. Steam uncovered for about 20 minutes. If necessary, add more water. When steam is released from the couscous, remove and transfer to a bowl.
- Pour 1/2 cup water and the remaining 115 g butter on the couscous and mix well. Place couscous in the steamer again and cover tightly. Steam for another 20–30 minutes. Transfer the couscous to a bowl. Pour some gravy over it and place vegetables and beef on top. Garnish with coriander leaves. Serve the extra gravy separately in a bowl.

Djej Matisha Mesla
(Honey Chicken with Almonds)

The Greeks love to use honey in their dessert pastries. In Morocco, honey is used to enhance the taste of nuts and dried fruits, including pistachios, walnuts, pine nuts, almonds, apricots, prunes, figs and raisins. The Persians, Arabs and Ottomans use nuts to make thick sauces and as food decorations. In this recipe, both honey and nuts are used to flavour the chicken.

Ingredients:

Chicken	1 (1.5 kg), cut into four pieces
Butter	3 Tbsp
Onion	1, peeled and grated
Ground cinnamon	2 tsp
Ground turmeric	$1/4$ tsp
Ground ginger	$1/4$ tsp
Garlic	1 clove, peeled and finely chopped
Ripe tomatoes	1.5 kg, peeled and finely chopped
Honey	2 Tbsp
Salt to taste	
Almonds	100 g, fried until golden brown
Sesame seeds	1 Tbsp, lightly roasted in the oven

Method:

- Put the chicken, butter, onion, cinnamon, turmeric, ginger, garlic and tomatoes in a pot. Cover and leave to simmer, stirring regularly and turning the chicken over once in a while. Cook until the chicken is tender. Test by inserting a skewer. The juices should run clear. Remove the chicken from the pot and place on a serving dish.
- Leave the sauce to simmer until it is thick and dark-coloured. Add the honey and salt. Stir.
- Pour the gravy over the chicken and garnish with almonds and sesame seeds. Serve.

Nach Bous
(Spicy Fried Prawns)

The Middle East is surrounded by the Mediterranean Sea, Black Sea, Red Sea, Caspian Sea and the Persian Gulf. The Nile, Tigris and Euphrates also flow through the Middle Eastern countries. As such, there is an abundant supply of seafood and many different ways of cooking it. In Turkey and Armenia, fish is usually baked with tomatoes, garlic and herbs. In Morocco, it is seasoned with *chermoula* (a paste made with various herbs and spices) and cooked in *tahini*. This Nach Bous recipe is popular in Kuwait, Bahrain and Saudi Arabia.

Ingredients:

Ghee	1 Tbsp
Onion	1, peeled and finely chopped
Garlic	4 cloves, peeled and finely chopped
Ground fennel	1 tsp
Ground turmeric	$1/2$ tsp
Fish curry powder	1 tsp
Chilli powder	1 tsp
Prawns (shrimps)	500 g medium, shelled and deveined
Coriander leaves (cilantro)	2 Tbsp, finely sliced
Salt to taste	
Lime juice	extracted from $1/2$ lime

Method:

- Heat ghee in a pan over moderate heat and sauté the onion and garlic until soft.
- Add the fennel, turmeric, curry powder and chilli powder and fry until fragrant. Stir in the prawns and continue to cook for a few minutes.
- Transfer to serving dish and sprinkle with coriander leaves, salt and lime juice. Serve with rice or bread.

Baklava

Baklava is a popular sweet pastry from the Middle East. This dessert uses a mixture of rose water, orange extracts, ground cinnamon and cloves, and produces a beautiful aroma.

Ingredients:

Syrup:

Castor sugar	500 g
Water	1½ cups
Cloves	5
Lemon juice	extracted from 1 lemon
Orange juice	extracted from 1 orange
Rose water	2 Tbsp

Baklava:

Mixed nuts (walnuts, hazelnuts, pistachios and almonds)	750 g, oven-roasted for 10 minutes and finely ground
Ground cinnamon	2 Tbsp
Unsalted butter	340 g, melted
Phyllo pastry	500 g

Method:

- Preheat the oven to 180°C.
- In a pot, mix the ingredients for the syrup and bring to boil for 10 minutes until it thickens. Strain the syrup and leave to cool.
- Mix the nuts with ground cinnamon in a bowl.
- Lightly grease a mould or baking tray with melted butter and line with a layer of phyllo pastry. Grease the phyllo pastry with melted butter and sprinkle with nuts. Repeat the process of layering until the pastry sheets are all used up. Brush the top layer with butter.
- Using a sharp knife, cut the pastry into diamond-shaped pieces. Bake at 180°C for 1 hour until lightly browned. Remove from the oven and pour the syrup on top. Allow the pastry to soak for a few hours before serving.

CHEF'S NOTE: *The baklava may be decorated with cloves. Use only half the portion of syrup if you do not like it too sweet. Individual slices can be served in paper cupcake cups.*

Wan-derings

MIDDLE EASTERN cooking is very sensual and aromatic. Its cuisine is flavoured with all kinds of fragrant ingredients, including garlic, saffron, cinnamon, chillies, fennel, coriander, jasmine, rose buds and orange extracts.

On my first visit to a market in Casablanca, Morocco, I was amazed at the variety of spices and herbs I saw! There were spices in different colours and there were twisted roots, grains, berries, dried plants, buds, petals and jars and jars of aromatic essences and oils! It took me three hours to examine and learn about the uses of these wonderful ingredients!

Mediterranean

Greece ❖ Italy ❖ Spain

Lekhadnodolmathes me Saltsa Domatas
(Cabbage Wrapped Beef and Tomato Sauce)

Greece is a haven for vegetable lovers. During the peak of the vegetable season, the markets are filled with colourful heaps of aubergines (eggplants), courgettes (zucchinis), chillies, carrots, potatoes, tomatoes, asparagus, artichokes, cucumbers and cabbages. Cabbages are very cheap in the winter months and they are great in salads and other family dishes. This recipe uses cabbage leaves and is one of the more popular dishes eaten in Greece.

Ingredients:

Cabbage	900 g
Olive oil	1/4 cup
Onion	1, peeled and diced
Minced (ground) beef	500 g
Allspice powder	1 tsp
Pine nuts	1/4 cup
Currants	1/4 cup
Cooked rice	1 1/2 cups
Salt and ground white pepper to taste	
Mint leaves	2 Tbsp, finely chopped
Lemon juice	extracted from 1 lemon
Tomato sauce	1 1/2 cups
Parsley leaves	1/4 cup, chopped as garnish

Method:
- Preheat the oven to 190°C.
- Peel and wash the cabbage leaves. Steam the leaves for 5 minutes until soft. Leave to cool. (Remove the spine for ease of wrapping.)
- In a pan, heat the olive oil and sauté the onion until soft and add the beef. Fry until dry. Add the allspice powder, pine nuts, currants, cooked rice, salt and ground white pepper. Stir-fry for a few minutes. Add the mint and parsley leaves and lemon juice. Remove from the pan.
- Spread out a piece of steamed cabbage leaf and place 1 Tbsp of beef filling in the centre. Wrap and arrange on a baking tray. Continue until all the beef filling has been used up.
- Pour the tomato sauce on top of the cabbage rolls and bake in the oven for half hour. Transfer to serving dish, garnish with chopped parsley and serve hot.

w a n - d e r i n g s

I HAD the opportunity to work in a number of Greek restaurants in Sydney and Vancouver and I learnt much about the cuisine from Chef Arthur, a chef at the Alexandria in Sydney, Australia.

I have since visited Greece twice and hold many fond memories about the place—its colours, views, aromas and tastes. The Greek philosophy concerning food is simple—make it fresh and aromatic and serve it hot. In Greece, a full spread of *mezethes* (appetisers) is usually laid out on the table as starters while waiting for other food to be served. While family and guests are enjoying the *mezethes*, the complete meal, from the breads to the salads and main courses, will then be brought out on large serving trays. Everybody enjoys the meal together.

A visit to the Greek markets is another wonderful experience. You will be fascinated by the multitude of colours and textures of its vegetables, fruits, cereals, grains, dried fruits, sausages, meats, fresh fish, salted fish and perhaps a hundred different types of olives and nuts that you may never have imagined! The variety is remarkable!

In the following pages, I will share with you some of the lovely recipes I acquired from working in the Greek restaurants. Some of these recipes are also contributions from my Greek acquaintances.

Arni Souvlakia me Pilafi
(Lamb Kebab and Rice)

This recipe originated from Turkey and is served as *mezzeh,* a starter or appetiser served before the main meal. For the full flavours to be soaked into the lamb, it should be left to marinate overnight. Thus when cooking this dish, do prepare a day ahead.

Ingredients:

Lamb	2 kg, cut into 5-cm cubes and seasoned with salt

Marinade:

Onion	1, peeled and quartered
Olive oil	1$\frac{1}{3}$ cups
Lemon juice	$\frac{1}{3}$ cup
Garlic paste	3 Tbsp
Fresh Oregano	3 Tbsp
Ground black pepper	2 Tbsp
Salt to taste	

Method:
- Blend the onion quarters in a blender until it becomes a fine paste. Add the other marinade ingredients into the blender one at a time and blend well.
- Season the lamb with the marinade and keep overnight in the refrigerator.
- The following day, remove the lamb from the marinade and skewer the meat. Sprinkle a little salt on the skewered meat.
- Grill (broil) the lamb until cooked. Serve with rice, potatoes, vegetables, cucumbers and tomatoes, if desired.

Rizogalo me Lemoni
(Lemon Rice Pudding)

Like the Turkish, the Greeks love their pastries, pies and cakes covered with generous portions of syrup. The pastry chefs also make special commemorative cakes for celebrations and festivals. Most of these desserts are laced with honey or syrup fragranced with orange flowers, rose water or aromatic spices. When I was in Athens and Crete Island, I bothered the staff in the pastry shops with so many questions about these desserts that I ended up buying boxes and boxes of sweets in appreciation!

I personally don't fancy anything too sweet but this Lemon Rice Pudding is not too sweet and truly refreshing. I love the lemon flavour and the aroma from the rose water.

Ingredients:

Fragrant rice	135 g
Water to boil the rice	
Lemon rind	grated from 1 lemon
Fresh milk	3 cups
Butter	1 Tbsp
Rose water	1 Tbsp
Vanilla essence	1/2 tsp
A pinch of salt	
Castor sugar	110 g, divided into 2 portions
Eggs	3, whites and yolks separated
Lemon juice	extracted from 1 lemon
Whipping cream	1/3 cup, beaten until fluffy
Icing (Confectioners') sugar	3 Tbsp

Method:

- Preheat the oven to 180°C. Prepare a mould and a deep baking tray large enough to place the mould in. Grease the mould with butter and set aside.
- Mix the rice, water and lemon rind in a pot and bring to the boil for 1–2 minutes. Strain the rice and discard the water. Add milk, butter, rose water and vanilla essence to the rice and bring to the boil. Add salt and half portion of sugar and cook over medium heat until the mixture thickens. When it is almost dry, remove from heat and cool.
- In a separate bowl, beat the egg yolks and lemon juice until fluffy. Add the beaten mixture and whipped cream to the cooled rice.
- In another bowl, combine the egg whites and remaining portion of sugar and beat until light and fluffy. Gradually add to the rice and mix well.
- Pour the rice mixture into the prepared mould. Even out the top and sift icing sugar over. Place the mould in the deep baking tray and pour boiling water around the mould, filling to about three quarter the height of the mould. Bake at for 20 minutes.

CHEF'S NOTE: *As a variation to the recipe, use oranges in place of lemons.*

Minestrone alla Milanese
(Milan Minestrone Soup)

It was this lovely soup that got me hooked to Italian cooking. It all started in January 1986 when one of my friends, Ned Bynner gave me two cookbooks—*The Talisman Italian Cookbook* and *The Joy of Cooking*. I had just arrived to study at the California Culinary Academy to fulfil my dream of becoming a chef. At that time, I knew very little about Italian cooking, except for dishes like meatball spaghetti, lasagne and pizza. One winter morning, I decided to try one of the Italian recipes and chose this particular one. It turned out wonderfully and we enjoyed the soup to the last drop. From there, I continued to make improvements to the recipe.

The soup is best made in summer when there are plenty of ripe tomatoes and fresh herbs. The soup can be frozen for later use and I find that it also tastes better over time! The secret in making this lovely soup is to always use good meat stock, vegetable and fresh herbs. There are many ways to prepare this soup. You can use all kinds of vegetables, but just be sure to add one or two types of starchy ingredients. Italians use beans, rice or pasta. Be sure also to add enough water or else the soup will thicken too quickly because of the starchy ingredients.

Ingredients:

Olive oil	1 tsp
Garlic	2 cloves, peeled and finely chopped
Onion	1/2, peeled and diced
Parsley leaves	2 Tbsp, chopped
Basil leaves	1 Tbsp
Tomato puree	1 Tbsp
Chicken stock	6³/₈ cups
Celery	3 stalks, diced
Carrots	2, peeled and diced
Potatoes	2, peeled and diced
Small cabbage	1/4, thickly sliced
Zucchinis (Courgettes)	2, diced
Macaroni	120 g
Parmesan cheese as garnish	

Method

- In a pan, heat the olive oil and sauté the garlic, onion, parsley and basil leaves until fragrant. Stir in tomato puree. Add chicken stock, celery, carrots, potatoes, cabbage and zucchinis and bring to the boil for 40 minutes.
- Stir in the macaroni and cook for another 10 minutes. Sprinkle Parmesan cheese on top and serve hot.

Insalata di Gamberetti e Peperoni Rossi
(Prawns and Capsicum Salad)

Seafood salad is very popular in Italy during the summer months, especially in the coastal towns. Nothing could be more tempting than a plate of fresh seafood tossed in olive oil and decorated with lemon and herbs!

For this recipe, large prawns (shrimps), sweet smoked chilli and oregano are combined to make a lovely salad. Prepare the complete salad and leave it in the fridge for an hour for the dressing to mature. However, this salad must be served at room temperature. You may serve it as an appetiser or side dish with crusty Italian bread rolls.

Ingredients:

Red capsicums (bell peppers)	3
Garlic	2 cloves, peeled and finely chopped
Parsley leaves	1 Tbsp, chopped
Oregano (preferably fresh)	1 tsp
Salt and ground black pepper to taste	
Lemon juice	extracted from 1 lemon
Olive oil	1/3 cup
Prawns (shrimps)	1 kg large, boiled for 2 minutes and drained
Black olives	1/2 cup

Method:
- Grill (broil) the whole capsicums, constantly turning to even out the cooking, until soft and the skin is black. Put the capsicums in a bowl and cover tightly with plastic food wrap. Leave for 10 minutes. Keeping the steam in this way will make it easy to remove the skin.
- Peel the skins and cut the capsicums in two. Remove the seeds and cut into strips.
- In a separate bowl, mix the garlic, parsley leaves, oregano, salt, ground black pepper and lemon juice and stir well with a spoon. Pour in the olive oil and stir until well combined.
- Add the prawns, capsicums and olives to the mixture. Mix well. Refrigerate and leave to marinate for 1 hour. This will allow the mixture to mature. Remove from refrigerator and leave for 10–15 minutes until salad is at room temperature. Serve with bread.

Insalata di Rinforzo col Cavolfiore
(Cauliflower and Red Chilli Salad)

Most people who have been to Italy and tasted Italian food enjoy the lovely taste of various Italian salads. Italian salads are neither too spicy nor too plain. The ingredients are simple and go well together. The Italians use only the best original olive oil and wine vinegar. Here is a tradisional salad recipe from Sicily. This salad is usually served during the Christmas and New Year celebrations.

Ingredients:

Cauliflower florets	600 g
Salt to taste	
Capers	2 Tbsp
Pickled anchovies	4, pounded to a fine paste
Red capsicums (bell peppers)	1, halved, seeded and sliced
Green olives	10, seeded and halved
Red wine vinegar	2 Tbsp
Pure olive oil	1/3 cup
Ground black pepper to taste	

Method:
- Boil a pot of water and add some salt. Blanch the cauliflower until soft. Drain and leave to cool.
- Combine the cauliflower with all the other ingredients in a bowl and stir well. Add salt and seasoning to taste.

CHEF'S NOTE: *Red wine vinegar may be replaced with prune juice.*

Scampi Con Pomodoro Fresco
(Fried Prawns with Tomatoes)

While holidaying in Italy, I had the opportunity to visit Venice for the first time. We had dinner at a very beautiful restaurant in Hotel Cipriani. I ordered this dish as a starter. The dish was beautifully presented and the ingredients were very fresh. I tried preparing a similar dish on my own and I realised that fresh prawns (shrimps) and ripe tomatoes are what gives this dish its wonderful taste.

Ingredients:

Olive oil	3 Tbsp
Ripe tomatoes	5, peeled, seeded and diced
Salt and ground white pepper to taste	
Unsalted butter	3 Tbsp
Garlic	2 cloves, finely chopped
Prawns (shrimps)	15 medium
Clear wine	1 cup
Parsley leaves	2 Tbsp, chopped as garnish

Method:

- In a pan, heat the olive oil and sauté the tomatoes until they are a little dry. Add salt and ground white pepper.
- In a separate saucepan, heat the butter and stir-fry the garlic until fragrant. Sauté the prawns. Pour in the clear wine and turn up the heat. Allow to boil until the liquid quantity is reduced by half. Add the tomatoes and prawns. Garnish with parsley and serve.

CHEF'S NOTE: *As an alternative to wine, use chicken stock.*

Polpettoncini alla Napoletana Fritti
(Beef Croquettes with Mozzarella)

Italian are experts in creating dishes with aubergines (eggplants). When grilled, the aubergine can be served as *antipasto* (appetiser)—*melanzane alla griglia*—or a main dish —*melanzane al forno*. Fried aubergine dipped in egg is known as *melanzane dorate*. Whichever way it is prepared, aubergine is simply delicious!

Ingredients:

Aubergines (eggplants)	2, sliced and grilled (broiled) until tender
Minced beef	600 g
Eggs	2, beaten
Bread	3 slices, soaked in water and drained
Parsley leaves	2 Tbsp, chopped
Parmesan cheese	45 g, grated
Mozzarella cheese	200 g, cut into small cubes
Onion	1, peeled, cut into small cubes and lightly fried in olive oil
Garlic	2 cloves, peeled, finely chopped and lightly fried in olive oil
Plain (all-purpose) flour	150 g
Cooking oil for frying	
Salt and ground white pepper to taste	

Method:
- Scoop out the flesh of the grilled aubergines and mash into a fine paste.
- Combine the beef, aubergines, beaten eggs, bread, parsley, Parmesan and Mozzarella cheese, onion and garlic. Shape into longish rolls.
- Coat the rolls in flour and fry until golden brown. Serve with lemon slices.

CHEF'S NOTE: *This dish can be served with Italian tomato sauce, the kind used as a base for pizza.*

Wan-derings

WHILE undergoing a pastry course in Paris, I decided to enrol for an additional two-month course at the reputable Marcella Hazan Culinary School. The fees were shockingly high but because my employer, Mr Gentry, was willing to sponsor the course, I went ahead with it. Within two months, I mastered many Italian cooking styles. This recipe is from the school.

To rid the aubergine of its bitter taste, sprinkle a little salt on the cut or sliced aubergines and set aside for one hour until the moisture dries up. Then pat them dry before cooking.

Pollo alla Milanese
(Fried Chicken Milan Style)

This simple chicken recipe is my foster father, Neil Mohanan's favourite. When I first went to stay with him in San Francisco, I wanted to prepare him something special for dinner but I did not know what he liked. I simply popped into a nearby supermarket and bought a can of seasoned breadcrumbs and some chicken. The chicken dish tasted so good that Neil asked for it all the time. I did not reveal the secret about the seasoned breadcrumbs to him, but as time passed, I managed to create my own Milanese chicken by preparing the seasoned breadcrumbs myself. I hope you will enjoy this recipe just as Neil did.

Ingredients:

Chicken breast	4 pieces (150 g each)
Salt and ground white pepper to taste	
Breadcrumbs	³/₄ cup
Parmesan cheese	50 g, grated
Parsley leaves	1 Tbsp, chopped
Egg	1
Fresh milk	¹/₂ cup
Olive oil	1 cup
Unsalted butter	2 Tbsp
Lemon juice	2 Tbsp
Parsley and lemon slices as garnish	

Method:

- Flatten the chicken breast to about 0.5-cm thickness between two pieces of greaseproof paper. Rub the chicken pieces with a little salt and ground white pepper.
- In a bowl, mix the breadcrumbs, Parmesan cheese and parsley leaves with a little salt and ground white pepper.
- In another bowl, beat the eggs and fresh milk. Dip the chicken in the mixture and roll in the breadcrumbs mixture. Do this one piece at a time.
- In a pan, heat the olive oil and fry the chicken breasts until golden brown on both sides. When chicken is cooked, transfer to a serving plate. Melt the butter in the same pan until little bubbles begin to appear. Stir in lemon juice and pour over the chicken breasts. Garnish with parsley and lemon slices and serve.

CHEF'S NOTE: *This dish goes well with boiled potatoes or pasta.*

Trota alla Griglia
(Grilled Trout)

There is nothing simpler or more nutritious than fresh fish grilled and dabbed with the best olive oil. People in the Mediterranean countries knew this secret decades ago. Today, more people are beginning to practise this simple way of cooking. Grilling or baking enhances the taste of fish and may even make it sweeter! However, the secret to a good fish dish lies in the freshness of the fish.

As fresh trouts are not easily available in Malaysia, you may have to settle for frozen ones from the supermarket. Alternatively, you may use *senangin,* a threadfin fish which I feel is similar in texture to the trout. This recipe comes from a small restaurant in the east coast of Sardinia Island. Seafood is a common menu item there, but the people of Sardinian island also love barbecued lamb.

Ingredients:

Butter	115 g
Fresh button mushrooms	300 g
Parsley leaves	2 Tbsp, chopped
Salt and ground black pepper to taste	
Trouts	4 medium
Salt	$1/4$ tsp
Ground white pepper	$1/2$ tsp
Plain (all-purpose) flour	75 g, sifted
Breadcrumbs	2 Tbsp
Olive oil	1 Tbsp
Spring onions (scallions)	3, thinly sliced
Lemon and tomato slices as garnish	

Method:

- Preheat the oven to 190°C.
- In a pan, heat the butter and sauté the mushrooms and parsley until the mushrooms are almost soft. Add salt and ground black pepper to taste. Lay the mushrooms and parsley evenly on a baking tray.
- Season the fish with salt and ground white pepper. Coat in plain flour. Heat some butter and fry the fish for about 1 minute until both sides are golden brown. Place the fish on the prepared baking tray.
- Sprinkle breadcrumbs over the fish and pour in the oil that was used for frying earlier. Grill for 7 minutes. When done, remove and place grilled fish on serving dish.
- Heat the olive oil with a little butter, sauté the spring onions until soft and pour over fish. Garnish with tomato and lemon slices and serve.

Osso Bucco Gremolata

This is one of the best Italian dishes I have created and it is my favourite. The secret to this dish lies in the wine (either red or white/clear), meat stock and fresh herbs. While undergoing a cooking course in Italy, a chef by the name of Bucco Gyoyanni explained to me that in order to make good osso bucco, beef shank must be used, preferably from the dairy cow. This is because the meat is more tender and will easily separate from the bone. Eating this dish is an unforgettable experience. It's like eating *tulang sumsum!*

Ingredients:

Whole beef shank	6 pieces
Salt and ground black pepper to taste	
Plain (all-purpose) flour	75 g, sifted
Olive oil	1/2 cup
Onions	1 1/2, peeled and cubed
Garlic	3 cloves, peeled and chopped
Carrot	1, peeled and diced
Coriander leaves (cilantro)	1 sprig, chopped
Tomato puree	1 Tbsp
Italian tomatoes	2 cans (225 g each)
Beef stock	4 cups, or 2 beef stock cubes dissolved in 4 cups boiling water
Fresh basil leaves	2 Tbsp, chopped
Fresh thyme	2 Tbsp, chopped
Fresh oregano	2 Tbsp, chopped
Clear wine	2 cups
Salt and ground white pepper to taste	

Method:

- Preheat the oven to 180°C.
- Season the beef shanks with salt and ground black pepper. Dust in plain flour.
- In a pot, heat the olive oil and fry the beef shanks until golden brown. Set aside.
- In the same pot (preferably a covered earthen pot), add olive oil and sauté onions, garlic, carrot and coriander leaves with tomato puree until carrots are soft. Add canned tomatoes, beef stock and herbs.
- Put in beef shanks and pour in clear wine. Bring to the boil for a few minutes. Add salt and ground white pepper to taste.
- Transfer the osso bucco to an oven dish, cover and cook for 3 hours. Serve with gremolata*, a garnish of parsley, lemon rind and garlic.

CHEF'S NOTE: *Chicken stock may be used as a substitute to wine.*

*Gremolata

Ingredients:

Lemon rind	grated from 2 lemons
Parsley	1 sprig, chopped
Garlic	4 cloves, peeled and finely chopped

Method:

- Put the ingredients in a bowl and mix well.
- Use as garnish.

Pizza

I often wonder what Italian cooking would be like without tomatoes. Tomatoes, olive oil, garlic, onions, and fresh herbs, such as basil and oregano make Italian cooking interesting and delicious. To the Italians, pizza is a general word for pie, tart or anything that is round in shape, flat and baked in the oven. Pizza originated from the Naples district. A good pizza does not need a lot of toppings. It only needs three things: a good dough, fresh ingredients and a hot oven. Here is a recipe for basic pizza dough and several topping ideas. I have also included some tips to creating your own pizza.

Basic Pizza Dough (30 cm)

Ingredients:

Fresh yeast	1 Tbsp
Sugar	1 tsp
Warm water	1 cup
Plain (all-purpose) flour	450 g, sifted
Salt	1/4 tsp
Olive oil	4 Tbsp

CHEF'S NOTE: *The pizza dough may also be kneaded in the food processor or cake mixer with a dough blade. To make a crispy pizza base, the oven temperature must be hot enough. When blending the yeast with warm water, the temperature of the water must not exceed 120°C. Too high a temperature kills the yeast. The dough may be prepared in the morning, left to rise throughout the day and baked later in the evening before serving.*

Method:
- Preheat the oven to 230°C.
- In a bowl, combine the yeast, sugar and half portion of warm water. Mix well. Leave in a warm place to proof for 10 minutes.
- Sift the plain flour and salt. Introduce into the yeast mixture and knead for 10 minutes until the dough is firm and elastic.
- Grease a bowl and the dough with olive oil. Place dough in bowl. Cover with a damp towel. Leave for 1 hour for dough to double.
- Punch dough with your fist to flatten it and knead for 5 minutes. Cover with the cloth again and allow dough to proof for half hour more. Punch and knead dough again. Divide dough into 2 portions, shape into balls and flatten. The pizza base is ready.

*Margherita Pizza

Ingredients:

Pizza base	(see recipe above)
Tomato sauce	1 cup (see Basic Pizza Tomato Sauce recipe on page 84)
Mozzarella cheese	85 g, grated
Dried Oregano	1 tsp
Parmesan cheese	30 g
Black olives	4–5, sliced

Method
- Preheat the oven to 230°C.
- Spread the tomato sauce evenly on the pizza base and arrange the other ingredients ending with the olives on top. Bake for 15 minutes.

Pizza

Basic Pizza Tomato Sauce

Ingredients:

Olive oil	4 Tbsp
Garlic	3 cloves, peeled
Anchovies	2 Tbsp, pounded to a paste
Italian tomatoes	2 cans, 225 g each, blended
Parsley leaves	1 sprig, chopped
Dried Basil leaves	1 tsp
Salt and ground white pepper to taste	

Method:

- In a pan, heat olive oil and sauté garlic. Add anchovies and cook for a few minutes. Add blended tomatoes, parsley and basil. Season with salt and ground white pepper. Cook until the mixture thickens. Spread on pizza base.

*Napoletana Pizza

Ingredients:

Pizza base	(see Basic Pizza Dough recipe on paghe 82)
Tomato sauce	(see Basic Pizza Tomato Sauce recipe above)
Ripe tomatoes	6, finely sliced
Garlic	1 clove, peeled and finely chopped
Dried Oregano	1 tsp
Mozzarella cheese	110 g, grated
Olive oil	1 Tbsp

Method:

- Preheat the oven to 230°C.
- Spread the tomato sauce evenly on the pizza base and arrange the other ingredients except olive oil on top.
- Drizzle with olive oil and bake for 15 minutes.

Budino di Patete e Mandarie
(Potato Custard)

When Marcella Hazan suggested we organise a cooking demonstration on this dish at a cooking school in Paris, I looked at the recipe and thought it was a mistake. We use potatoes in soups and main dishes and I never thought it would be suitable for use in desserts. According to Marcella, the recipe was from Andte, a chef in a small restaurant in Bologna. Marcella was initially also rather hesitant about the idea. But you will soon find out what we did to the ordinary potato!

Ingredients:

Milk	2 cups
Potatoes	225 g, peeled and finely grated
Castor sugar	330 g
Water	1/4 cup
Egg whites	2
Egg yolks	4
Almonds	115 g, peeled and finely chopped
Lemon rind	grated from 3 lemons
Amaretto	1 1/2 tsp

Method:

- Preheat the oven to 190°C.
- Bring the milk to the boil and add grated potatoes. Stir and allow to boil for 5 minutes. Pour into a bowl and leave to cool.
- Add 110 g sugar with 1/4 cup water in another pot and cook to resemble golden caramel. Pour caramel into a round mould 7.5-cm deep and 20-cm wide. Spread caramel evenly on the base and the sides of the mould.
- Beat the eggs with 220 g sugar until fluffy. Add almonds, lemon rind and amaretto. Mix well. Add the potato mixture and mix well.
- Pour the mixture into the prepared mould and place in a 10-cm deep and 25-cm wide baking tray. Pour boiling water into the baking tray and bake for 1 hour in the oven.
- When the potato custard is done, leave to cool for a few hours. To remove the custard from the mould, heat the bottom of the mould for a few minutes. Place a plate over it and turn the mould over. The custard will fall onto the plate.

CHEF'S NOTE: *Amaretto is a kind of wine made from almonds. It may be substituted with 1/2 tsp almond essence.*

Pere Cotte Con
(Alloro Fragrant Pear)

This is a simple fruit dessert where the pear is cooked in syrup seasoned with cinnamon, clove and orange peel. The result is quite dramatic. You eat it with a scoop of Mascarpone cheese. You may also cook it in red or white wine, simmering it slowly until the wine evaporates and a thick syrup forms. However, you may also serve it in regular syrup.

This recipe requires overnight refrigeration. Allow greater lead time for yourself when preparing this recipe.

Ingredients:

Hard pears	6, peeled
Water	3 cups
Orange juice	2 Tbsp
Castor sugar	220 g
Vanilla essence	1 tsp
Lime rind	grated from 1 lime
Cinnamon sticks	2
Cloves	6

Method:

- Put the ingredients in a pot and bring to the boil. Turn the heat down and allow syrup to simmer and pears to cook evenly for 20 minutes. Cover the pot to prevent pears from bobbing up.
- Pierce the pears with a knife to test if they are soft. When soft, turn off the heat. Pour the syrup and pears into a bowl and leave to cool.
- When cool, refrigerate overnight to allow the mixture to mature. Serve cold.

CHEF'S NOTE: *Apples may be used in place of pears.*

Purrusalda
(Potato and Leek Soup)

The name of this soup is derived from a combination of words—leek, *puerros* and *saldo* which means *balanced*. It is also one of the names of Basque's local dance. Sometimes *balcao* or salted cod fish is added to this soup. The salted fish is first soaked and fried briefly. You may use grouper as an alternative to *balcao*.

Ingredients:

Butter	3 Tbsp
Leeks	6 stems (each 15-cm long from the base), thinly sliced
Potatoes	4 medium, peeled and sliced into rounds 1.5-cm thick
Garlic	2 cloves, finely chopped
Chicken stock	3 cups
Salt and ground white pepper to taste	

Method:
- Melt butter in a pan. Add leeks and stir-fry briefly until soft. Add potatoes, garlic and chicken stock. Cook for 20 minutes until potatoes are tender.
- Add salt and ground white pepper to taste. Serve hot.

CHEF'S NOTE: *This soup can be served with toasted or crusty bread. If desired, add 1/2 cup thick cream and blend the ingredients in a food processor until smooth to make a cream soup.*

Gazpacho

Tomato soup is the signature dish of the district of Andalusia. During the summer months in Andalusia, this soup is usually served cold. In Malaysia, we prefer our soup hot. Perhaps we should try something different once in a while.

Ingredients:

Ripe tomatoes	2 kg, cut into small cubes
Water	3 cups
Onion	1, peeled and cut into small cubes
Capsicums (bell peppers)	1¹/₂, cut into small cubes
Garlic	3 cloves, peeled and finely chopped
Clear wine	³/₄ cup
Tomato puree	6 Tbsp
Red wine vinegar	3 Tbsp
Salt and seasoning powder to taste	
French loaf	200 g, remove the crust, cut into small cubes and lightly fried in butter
Hardboiled eggs	2, peeled
Cucumber	1, peeled and cut into small cubes

Method:
- Put tomatoes, water, onion, capsicums, garlic, wine, tomato puree and vinegar in a food processor and blend until fine.
- Pour the blended mixture into a glass bowl and stir in salt and seasoning. Refrigerate for 2 hours.
- Serve with croutons (bread cubes lightly fried in butter until crispy), boiled eggs and cucumber cubes.

CHEF'S NOTE: *This soup is very nutritious as it is made from a variety of vegetables. Since we drink tomato, celery and carrot juices raw and cold, why not this? For those who cannot take wine, chicken stock may be used as a substitute. Red wine vinegar may also be replaced with prune juice.*

Ensalada Gambas De Naranja
(Prawns, Orange and Olive Salad with Sherry Vinaigrette)

The Spanish love eating olives and they may eat it every day! When a person is loved by many, this person is said to be *la suerte de las aceitunas* or having the luck of an olive.

There are many different types of olives available. Black olives are sold in their original form, while green olives are first seeded and filled with *pimiento* (red chilli), almond, anchovies or red onions. Today, Spain is the world's largest producer and exporter of olive fruit and olive oil.

Olives are the main snack in many tapas bars and cafés in Spain. It is used in salads, egg dishes, stews and sauces. This is of my favourite salads. It is simple, refreshing and combines all the elements of Spain. Serve this salad to your family and guests and perhaps you will be *la suerte de las aceitunas!*

Ingredients:

Sherry wine vinegar or clear wine vinegar	3 Tbsp
Garlic	1 clove, peeled and finely chopped
Sugar	1 tsp
Lime rind	1 tsp, grated
Salt and ground white pepper to taste	
Olive oil	1/4 cup
Oranges	2, peeled and cut into small cubes
Prawns (shrimps)	300 g medium, blanched and shelled
Pickled green olives	170 g
Lettuce leaves and spring onions as garnish	

Method:

- Mix the sherry wine vinegar, garlic, sugar, lime rind, salt and ground white pepper in a bowl. Stir. Pour in the olive oil and continue stirring until the mixture is well combined.
- Add the orange cubes, prawns and olives and mix well. Leave to marinade for 1 hour in the refrigerator.
- Arrange the salad on a plate lined with lettuce leaves and sprinkle with spring onions.

Guiso de Patatas Con Puntillitas
(Potato and Squid Stew)

When I was in Madrid, I would dine at different restaurants every day to try them out. The most memorable restaurant was the Taberna de Antonio Sanchez. This restaurant-cum-tapas bar was named after its owner, a famous matador in the 1920s. Many photos of famous matadors plaster the walls of the restaurant. The food served was delicious and I loved this particular dish that I ordered. I managed to persuade one of the waiters to get the recipe from the chef. To my surprise, the chef gladly gave me the recipe. Preparing this dish is simple and the flavour can be further enhanced by adding saffron and using good wine.

Ingredients:

Olive oil	3 Tbsp
Onion	1, peeled and finely chopped
Garlic	2 cloves, peeled and finely chopped
Green capsicums (bell peppers)	2, sliced
Tomatoes	2, seeded and finely sliced
Bay leaf	1
Clear wine	1/2 cup
Potatoes	3, peeled and cut into small cubes
Saffron strands	1 tsp
Fish stock	1 1/2 cups
Squid	600 g, cleaned and sliced into rings
Salt and ground white pepper to taste	

Method:

- In a pan, heat the olive oil and sauté onion, garlic and green capsicums briefly. Add the tomatoes and bay leaf and stir-fry for 2 minutes. Pour in the clear wine and simmer for another 3 minutes until the liquid quantity is reduced by half.
- Stir in potatoes, saffron strands and fish stock. Simmer until potatoes are soft. Add squid, salt and ground white pepper and stir for about 1–2 minutes before serving. Do not overcook the squid as it will make the squid elastic and tough to eat.

CHEF'S NOTE: *Usually when I mention fish stock, people moan thinking that there is so much to be done. But in actual fact, it is rather easy. The stock is the secret to a delicious meal and all you have to do is boil the bones or head of a fish such as the red snapper. You may even use prawn shells. Then put in some celery, onion, carrot, bay leaves and several black peppercorns. If you wish to use wine, drizzle a little into the stock. Then leave to simmer at low heat for 20 minutes and strain the stock. Here's a tip for preparing stock: make sure that the heat is kept really low as high heat may cause the stock to boil and form a layer of scum. Any leftover stock can be kept in the refrigerator for use later.*

Chicken stock may be used as a substitute to wine.

Fricando De langoscanos
(Prawns and Mushrooms with Almond Sauce)

This dish requires the ingredients to be marinated overnight. Make provision for more time when preparing this dish. However, the full flavours and taste of the wine and herbs absorbed by the prawns make it well worth the time!

Ingredients:

Onions	2, peeled and finely sliced
Garlic	1 clove, peeled and diced
Carrot	1, peeled and finely sliced
Clear wine	¼ cup
Bay leaf	1
Dried Thyme	¼ tsp
A pinch of ground cinnamon	
A dash of ground black pepper	
Salt to taste	
Fresh water prawns (shrimps)	350 g, medium, halved lengthwise with shell
Plain (all-purpose) flour	1 Tbsp, sifted
Olive oil	2 Tbsp
Tomato	1, thickly sliced
Fish or prawn stock stock	½ cup
Fresh button mushrooms	4, quartered
Almonds	1 Tbsp, finely blended

Method:

- Mix onions, garlic, carrots, wine, bay leaf, thyme, ground cinnamon, ground black pepper, salt and prawns in a bowl. Leave to marinate in the refrigerator overnight.
- The following day, strain the ingredients to remove any juices. Set the juice aside.
- Dry the prawns with a clean cloth or kitchen towel and coat with plain flour.
- Heat the olive oil in a pan and fry the prawns for 1 minute. Remove from heat.
- Put the other marinated ingredients in the pan and stir-fry until soft. Add more olive oil if necessary. Add tomato and stir-fry for a few minutes. Pour in the marinade juice and fish stock. Boil for 10 minutes until the mixture thickens. Remove the vegetables to a serving dish. Add the mushrooms, almonds and prawns and stir for 1–2 minutes. Transfer to dish of vegetables and serve.

CHEF'S NOTE: *For those who cannot take wine, chicken stock may be used as a substitute.*

wan-derings

TAPAS have been a favourite item for me since I discovered it when I visited Spain a few years ago. I love trying all sorts of food and since I was travelling on a tight budget, I found the tapas an ideal and inexpensive way to sample Spanish food. It's difficult to describe what tapas really is, as it is not a type of food but rather a reflection of the Spanish lifestyle and their way of eating. Tapas consists of a variety of dishes depending on the chef. It may be a starter or even the first course or main meal.

In Spanish culture, you don't entertain guests at home. Instead people meet at restaurants and tapas bars. The tapas bar is also the place for a quick bite before dinner. In this country where lunch is usually served between 2pm and 3pm and dinner at 10pm, tapas are an essential snack.

I always go to the tapas bars that are filled with Spanish people. They appreciate good food and bars that are packed with Spanish people mean they are really good! I have known this for a fact and I avoid the bars that are packed with tourists.

In the following pages are some tapas recipes you can try on your own. You may combine them with a selection of Malaysian cocktails for a Malaysian-style tapas festival!

Pimientos En Vinagre
(Pickled Capsicums)

These pickled capsicums (bell peppers) are very popular at tapas bars. Grilling (Broiling) the capsicums over glowing charcoal or on an electric grill gives the capsicums a wonderful and unique taste. Leave capsicums to grill till the skin is black. This will not burn the flesh inside. The capsicums need to be left to pickle overnight. Prepare this recipe a day ahead.

Ingredients:

Red capsicums (bell peppers)	3

Pickle:

Ground *paprika*	1/2 tsp
Water	1 Tbsp
Red wine vinegar	2 Tbsp
Dried Thyme	1/2 tsp
Garlic	1 clove, peeled and chopped
Onion	1, finely chopped
Parsley leaves	1 tsp , finely sliced
Bay leaf	1
Olive oil	1 Tbsp

Method:

- Preheat the oven to 180°C.
- Grill (broil) the capsicums for 25 minutes until soft. Remove and place in a covered bowl to prevent the steam from escaping. Leave for 10 minutes. This will make peeling the skin of the capsicums much easier.
- Halve the capsicums. Remove seeds and slowly remove skin. Do not wash the capsicums after they are cooked as they will loose their flavour. Pat dry with a paper towel. Set aside.
- In a separate bowl, blend the paprika with a little water and stir in red wine vinegar, thyme, garlic, onion, parsley and bay leaves and olive oil. Add capsicums and pickle overnight before serving.

CHEF'S NOTE: *Red wine vinegar may be substituted with prune juice.*

Albondigas Caseras
(Beef Balls)

It's no wonder this is another favourite tapas item. The combination of spices gives a wonderful flavour to the beef balls, while the breadcrumbs add bite.

Ingredients:

Minced beef	500 g
Breadcrumbs	50 g
Garlic	3 cloves, peeled and finely chopped
Eggs	2
Ground nutmeg	1/2 tsp
Salt	2 tsp
Ground black pepper	3/4 tsp
Plain (all-purpose) flour	150 g
Olive oil	3 Tbsp
Onion	1, peeled and finely chopped
Green capsicum (bell pepper)	1, finely sliced
Tomatoes	2, cubed
Clear wine (optional)	1/2 cup
Chicken stock	3/4 cup
Salt and ground white pepper to taste	
Parsley leaves	1 sprig, finely chopped

Method:

- Combine beef, beadcrumbs, garlic, eggs, nutmeg, salt and ground black pepper in a bowl. Mix well.
- Shape the mixture into small balls and coat with plain flour.
- Heat the olive oil and fry the beef balls until golden brown. Set aside to drain.
- Leave 1 Tbsp of olive oil in the pan and sauté the onion and green capsicum until almost soft. Stir in tomatoes, clear wine, chicken stock, salt and ground white pepper. Cover and bring to the boil for 45 minutes until mixture thickens.
- Pour sauce over beef balls, garnish with chopped parsley and serve.

CHEF'S NOTE: *The clear wine may be omitted from the recipe for those who prefer not to take wine.*

Ensaladilla Rusa
(Tuna and Vegetable Salad)

This is a type of potato salad with carrots and peas. It is sometimes mixed with tuna and boiled eggs and tossed in mayonnaise. This salad is one of the most popular Spanish tapas selections. It is usually served as it is, but is sometimes also used as a filling for pies and tarts.

Ingredients:

Potatoes	300 g, preferably new red potatoes
Red wine vinegar	1½ tsp
Onion	2 Tbsp, peeled and finely chopped
Garlic	1 clove, peeled and finely chopped
Parsley leaves	1 sprig, finely chopped
Capers	1 tsp, finely chopped
Pickled cornichon	2 Tbsp, finely sliced
Pimiento	1 Tbsp, coarsely sliced
Mayonnaise	½ cup
Salt and ground white pepper to taste	
Canned tuna	250 g, drained
Eggs	2, boiled, shelled and finely chopped
Green peas	3 Tbsp, precooked
Carrot	1, peeled, cubed and precooked to obtain 3 Tbsp.

Method:

- Boil the potatoes with a little salt. When tender, skin and cut into small cubes.
- In a bowl, mix the red wine vinegar, onion, garlic, parsley leaves, capers, pickled cornichon and pimiento with mayonnaise. Add salt and ground white pepper to taste. Stir in tuna, boiled potatoes, eggs, peas and carrots. Allow to sit for a few hours before serving.

CHEF'S NOTE: *For those who do not take red wine vinegar may be substituted with prune juice.*

Tortilla Espanola
(Spanish Potato Omelette)

Potato omelette is a favourite among the Spanish. This omelette is thicker and richer compared to the French omelette. In Spain, farmers and school-going children pack this potato omelette for lunch. This recipe is easy to prepare and tastes great too.

Ingredients:

Olive oil	1/2 cup
Onion	1, peeled and cut into small cubes
Potatoes	6, peeled, half-boiled and thinly sliced
Eggs	6
Salt and ground white pepper and to taste	
Parsley leaves	1 sprig, chopped

Method:

- Heat the olive oil in a pan. Fry the onion and potatoes until soft. Transfer onion and potatoes to a bowl and leave to cool.
- Beat the eggs with a little salt and white pepper. Add the potatoes, onion and parsley leaves to the beaten eggs and pour the mixture into the heated pan. Fry over low heat until the omelette starts to form. Do not increase the heat. Flip the omelette over and cook until slightly browned.
- Serve with cut lettuce, tomatoes and cucumber.

England ❖ France

Scones

Scones are a favourite item for afternoon tea in English homes. They are lovely when eaten hot with butter, whipped cream and strawberry jam. If you are preparing scones in large quantities, store them in the refrigerator and warm them in the oven when needed. Scones are easy to make and take only 15–20 minutes to prepare. Preparing the dough quickly helps, as this would allow the raising agent to take effect as soon as possible in the hot oven.

When making scones, the dough should be moist, soft and easy to roll and cut. Add more flour if the dough is too soft and add water a little at a time if the dough is too hard. Most scone recipes use too much bicarbonate of soda, which raises the dough quickly but also leaves the scones tasting of the powder. Good scone recipes use a combination of bicarbonate of soda and cream of tartar. This gives the scones a better taste.

Basic Scones

Ingredients:

Plain (all-purpose) flour	300 g, sifted
Bicarbonate of soda	1 tsp
Cream of tartar	2 tsp
A pinch of salt	
Butter	130 g, cut into small pieces
Fresh milk	3/4 cup
Egg	1, beaten

*Devonshire Cream

Thick creams may not be readily available in Asian countries. Here's a recipe for mock Devonshire cream that tastes like the real thing!

Ingredients:

Whipping cream	1/2 cup
Icing (confectioner's) sugar	2 Tbsp
Sour cream	1/2 cup

Method:
- In a chilled mixing bowl, whisk cream until fluffy and gradually fold in icing sugar. Add sour cream and stir well.

Method for making Basic Scones:
- Preheat the oven to 230°C. Grease a baking tray lightly with butter.
- Sift together the flour, bicarbonate of soda, cream of tartar and salt.
- Using your fingers, rub the butter into the flour mixture until it resembles breadcrumbs. Add milk and mix well.
- Roll out the dough into a sheet 1.5-cm thick and cut to the desired shape. Arrange on baking tray and glaze with beaten egg. Bake for 15–20 minutes.
- Serve warm with butter, fruit jam and/or Devonshire Cream*.

Honey Scones

To make Honey Scones, use the Basic Scone recipe but reduce fresh milk to 1/2 cup and add 1/4 cup orange juice, 2 Tbsp honey, lemon rind from 1 lemon and 1 Tbsp chopped walnuts to the mixture.

Cream Scones

To make Cream Scones, use the Basic Scone recipe and substitute fresh milk with 3/4 cup fresh thick cream and add 2 beaten eggs.

Cheese Scones

To make Cheese Scones, use the Basic Scone recipe and mix 100 g grated cheese into the dough before rolling out. Use the cheddar cheese as it imparts a wonderful taste. Serve hot with vegetable soup or any cream soup.

Pratie Scones

Pratie is the term for *potato* in several parts of Ireland and Scotland. This flat scone is similar to a pancake and uses potatoes as its main ingredient. Pratie scones are best eaten hot.

Ingredients:

Potatoes	200 g, peeled, boiled and mashed while hot
Butter	1/3 cup, melted
Salt	1 tsp
Plain (all-purpose) flour	75 g, sifted

W a n -derings

I ALWAYS look forward to the relaxed atmosphere of Sunday afternoon teas. For me, afternoon tea is a time to enjoy the company of relatives and friends while savouring delicious spreads after a hard week of work.

When I was living abroad, I loved to prepare the afternoon tea. I did not mind making the extra effort to set the table—laying out my favourite silver or chinaware and folding pretty lace napkins. I also enjoyed making scones, sandwiches, tarts, cakes and cookies. In addition to these traditional English teatime favourites, I would also prepare Asian snacks such as curry puffs and spring rolls. These afternoon teas were very meaningful occasions for me and my guests would sometimes linger to chat into the night.

Should you be preparing afternoon tea for the family, don't forget to include a variety of cakes for the children. I hope the following recipes will provide you with some ideas to create your own delicious spread for afternoon teas.

Method:
- Combine ingredients in a mixing bowl to form dough. Knead dough on a pastry board sprinkled with flour. Divide dough into 3 portions.
- Shape into balls and flatten into 0.5-cm thick rounds.
- In a pan, heat some cooking oil and cook the pratie scones over medium heat. Cook each side for 5 minutes. Serve hot.

CHEF'S NOTE: *In Scotland,* pratie scones *are sometimes served at room temperature like bread.*

English Cucumber Sandwiches

I used to manage Angelica's Café & Restaurant in Honolulu. It is a restaurant famous for its afternoon tea selections and variety of sandwich spreads. From my stint there, I learnt that the ideal tea sandwich bread must be thin and neat. The filling should be spread thinly just to whet the diner's appetite for other snacks like scones, cakes and biscuits. In order to cut the bread thinly, the knife used must be very sharp. If you find the slices too thick, you can flatten them with a rolling pin.

There are a variety of classic English sandwiches for afternoon tea. You may have watercress, egg, cucumber, jam, cheese, tomato, smoked salmon, chicken and the list goes on. Sometimes, I just prefer the simple Cucumber Sandwich.

Ingredients:

Butter or margarine	100 g
Whipping cream	3 Tbsp, whisked until fluffy
English mustard	1 tsp
Salt and ground white pepper to taste	
Cucumber	1, peeled and thinly sliced
Lemon juice	2 tsp
Olive oil	1 Tbsp
White bread	12 slices

Method:

- Cream the margarine or butter until light and fluffy. Mix in the whipped cream, English mustard, salt and ground white pepper.
- Season the cucumber slices with a little salt. Set aside in a strainer for 1 hour.
- After 1 hour, squeeze the excess water from the cucumber slices and mix them with lemon juice, olive oil and ground white pepper.
- Spread the margarine mixture on one side of each slice of bread. Arrange the cucumber slices on the bread and cover with another slice of bread. Cut into smaller pieces.

CHEF'S NOTE: *When preparing cucumber sandwiches, try not to prepare them too early as the bread may become soggy.*

Dundee Cake

A Dundee cake is a Scottish fruitcake. Although it is not a Christmas cake, I sometimes prepare it during festive seasons as a gift for friends. I read that the Dundee cake was created long before pitted raisins were introduced. Thus, the raisins had to be pitted manually before use! I cannot imagine spending all that time taking out all those seeds!

This recipe was originally from a magazine I read when I was 10 years old. I have since modified and made improvements to it over the years. I hope you enjoy it as much as I do.

Ingredients:

Sultanas (seedless white raisins)	150 g, chopped
Raisins	75 g
Butter	375 g
Castor sugar	170 g
Eggs	3
Plain (all-purpose) flour	350 g, sifted
Baking powder	1 tsp
Salt	1/2 tsp
Fresh milk	1/2 cup
Orange rind	grated from 1 orange
Almonds	35 g, ground
Almonds for decoration	10–12

Method:

- Preheat the oven to 160°C.
- Grease a 23-cm wide cake tin with butter and line with greaseproof baking paper. Set aside.
- Combine the sultanas and raisins and set aside.
- Cream together the butter and sugar until light and fluffy. Add eggs, one at a time, beating well after each addition.
- In another bowl, sift together flour, baking powder and salt. Fold into the creamed mixture a little at a time. Alternate this with milk a little at a time. Make sure that the batter is well blended but not over-beaten.
- Stir in the fruits, orange rind and ground almonds. Pour into the cake tin and decorate the top with whole almonds. Bake for 1 1/4 hours or until the sides leave the tin.

Irish Black Ginger Cake

Irish Black Ginger Cake is a traditional English cake. This recipe belongs to my foster father's aunt who lived in a small fishing village in Cork County, south of Ireland. This cake is rather compact and dark and looks like a chocolate cake without the chocolate! It is however very rich in ginger and molasses, and tastes good plain. You may also sandwich or coat the cake with cream cheese.

Ingredients:

Butter	250 g, softened
Castor sugar	110 g
Egg	1
Black molasses	1 cup
Plain (all-purpose) flour	375 g, sifted
Ground cinnamon	1½ tsp
Ground cloves	1 tsp
Ground ginger	1 tsp
Salt	½ tsp
Baking powder	1½ tsp
Thick coffee	1 cup, hot

Method:

- Preheat the oven to 180°C. Grease a 23-cm wide round cake tin with some butter.
- Cream the butter and sugar until light and fluffy. Mix in the egg and black molasses.
- In another bowl, sift the plain flour, cinnamon, cloves, ginger and salt together. Fold into the batter and mix well.
- Stir the baking powder into the hot coffee and pour into the batter. Mix well and pour into the cake tin.
- Bake for 45 minutes to 1 hour. Insert a skewer into the centre of the cake to test if it is done. If the skewer comes out clean, the cake is done. Serve plain or with cream cheese.

Orange Shortbread

Shortbread is a buttery biscuit originating from Scotland. This biscuit can be cut into several traditional shapes. I got this recipe from Noel, a Scottish pastry chef, while we were working in Vancouver, Canada.

You may make the dough and store it in the refrigerator for use later. But be forewarned. Shortbreads are addictive and the ones from this recipe definitely are!

Ingredients:

Unsalted butter	450 g
Demerara sugar	330 g
Orange essence	1 tsp
Orange rinds	grated from 2 oranges
Eggs	2, beaten
Plain (all-purpose) flour	600 g, sifted
A pinch of salt	
Egg for glacing	1, beaten with 2 Tbsp water

Method:
- Preheat the oven to 180°C. Grease a baking tray with some butter and set aside.
- Cream butter and demerara sugar until fluffy. Add in orange essence and grated orange rind. Slowly stir in the beaten eggs, flour and salt. Mix well.
- Roll out the dough on a sheet of greaseproof baking paper and set aside in the refrigerator for 2 hours.
- Place the chilled dough on a pastry board dusted with flour and roll out until the dough is about 1-cm thick. Cut out the desired shapes and place on the prepared baking tray. Brush the shortbread with egg-and-water mixture and prick the top of each cookie lightly with a fork before baking for 15–20 minutes until golden brown. Bake for another few minutes if you prefer the cookies to be more crisp.

CHEF'S NOTE: *Some people prefer their shortbreads to be thick while others enjoy them thin and crispy. You may vary the thickness of the shortbread according to your personal preference. Thicker shortbread may require a longer baking time.*

Onion Tart

I had tea in a small restaurant facing the Thames in London several years ago. I ordered a delicious Petal Onion Tart. It was so good that I had to try making it on my own when I returned to Malaysia. This Onion Tart recipe is similar to the one I had in London.

Ingredients:

Pastry:

Plain (all-purpose) flour	250 g, sifted
A pinch of salt	
Butter	170 g, chilled and cut into small pieces
Egg	1, lightly beaten
Water, if required	

Filling:

Butter	4 Tbsp
Onions (preferably white)	6 medium, peeled and thinly sliced
Water	1 Tbsp
A pinch of salt, ground white pepper and sugar	

Custard:

Eggs	2
Egg yolks	2
A pinch of salt, ground white pepper, sugar and ground nutmeg	
Fresh milk	1 cup
Whipped cream	1 cup

Method:

For the pastry:

- Combine the flour and salt and rub in the butter quickly until the mixture resembles breadcrumbs. Add egg and blend well. If necessary, add water to make a soft dough.
- Shape the dough into balls. Refrigerate for 30 minutes.
- Roll out the pastry into a 1 cm-thick sheet and press it into a greased tart tin. Bake in the oven at 180°C for 5 minutes.

For the filling:

- Heat the butter in a pan and add onions, water, salt, ground white pepper and sugar. Cover the pan and simmer for 20 minutes, stirring occasionally.
- When the onions are golden brown and very soft, remove from heat and cool. Set aside.

For the custard:

- In a bowl, beat the eggs, egg yolks, salt, white pepper, nutmeg, milk and whipped cream until well combined.

Preparing the tart:

- Fill the half-baked pastry crust with the filling. Pour in the custard and bake for 15–20 minutes. Serve hot.

English Trifle

The secret in making good custard lies in the quality of the ingredients and in using low and stable heat. I love this recipe because it is easy and there are no specific rules to preparing it. This is a recipe where you can put just about anything and the end-result is just amazing! To allow the beautiful and colourful trifle layers to be seen, clear and colourless glass bowls and glasses are ideal.

Ingredients:

Custard*	1 portion (see recipe below)
Sponge cake or pound cake	1, 28 x 46 cm
Lemon custard**	2 cups (see recipe below)
Brandy (optional)	1/2 cup
Strawberries	3 cups, cut into small pieces
Blueberries	3 cups
Whipping cream	1 cup, whisked with 2 tsp sugar until light and fluffy

Mint leaves as decoration

*Custard

Ingredients:

Evaporated milk	2⁵/8 cups
Whipped cream	1 cup
Vanilla essence	1 Tbsp
Eggs	4
Castor sugar	170 g
Corn flour (corn starch)	1/4 cup
A pinch of salt	
Unsalted butter	2 Tbsp

Method:
- Heat the milk, cream and vanilla essence in a saucepan and leave to simmer.
- Fill another pan half full with water and bring to the boil.
- In a stainless steel bowl, beat the eggs and castor sugar until fluffy. Add corn flour and mix well. Pour in the warm milk mixture a little at a time, stirring well each time.
- Place the bowl in the pan of boiling water and leave the custard to cook and thicken, stirring occasionally to prevent the bottom layer from sticking to the base. Stir in butter and mix until well blended. Remove the bowl. Leave the custard to cool for a few hours before using.

Method:
- Cut the cake into 2.5 X 1-cm pieces. Set aside.
- Spread 1 Tbsp each of custard and lemon custard at the base of a glass bowl. Arrange pieces of cake side by side until a base layer is formed. Drizzle some brandy (optional) on the cake and add another layer of lemon custard.
- Arrange fruits on top and add another layer of custard. Repeat the process until all the custard is used up, leaving some fruits for decorating the top. Decorate the top layer with the remaining fruits and mint leaves.
- Refrigerate the trifle for at least 4 hours before serving. If time allows, refrigerate overnight to allow the cake to mature. Pipe with whipped cream and serve.

CHEF'S NOTE: *Besides strawberries and blueberries, local fruits like pineapples, papaya, mangoes or bananas can also be used. Canned fruits like apricots may also be blended in the food processor and layered with melted chocolate. Adding durian flesh to the custard also makes it really tasty.*

**Lemon Custard

Ingredients:

Castor sugar	440 g
A pinch of salt	
Egg yolks	5
Eggs	3
Lemon juice	1 cup
Unsalted butter	5 Tbsp

Method:

- Fill a pan half full with water and bring to the boil.
- Prepare a basin of cold water. Set aside.
- In a bowl, mix together the castor sugar and salt. Add egg yolks and beat. Continue beating while adding the eggs one at a time. Add lemon juice and place the bowl into the pan of boiling water. Add the butter a little at a time, stirring continuously until it is well mixed. When the mixture begins to thicken and sticks to the back of the spoon, remove from heat and cool immediately in the basin of cold water.

CHEF'S NOTE: *The lemon custard may be kept for several weeks in the refrigerator. You may prepare the custard and lemon custard a day before making the trifle.*

Cinnamon Rolls

When there is some leftover pastry from making pies, I enjoy using it to make cinnamon rolls. Sometimes. I will add chopped nuts, raisins (sultanas) or dates. This is great as breakfast or a teatime treat.

Ingredients:

Butter	6 Tbsp, softened
Puff pastry*	1 portion (see recipe below)
Castor sugar	150 g
Ground cinnamon	1 Tbsp
Raisins	1 cup

Method:

- Preheat the oven to 200°C. Grease a baking tray with some butter. Set aside.
- Roll out the pastry into a 25 x 35 cm sheet, 1-cm thick.
- In a bowl, mix together the sugar and ground cinnamon. Spread the mixture all over the pastry sheet. Sprinkle with raisins.
- Roll the pastry up from one side until the whole sheet is rolled up like a jelly roll. Cut the roll into 2.5-cm thick slices. Arrange on baking tray. Bake for 10–12 minutes. Cool and serve.

*Puff Pastry

Ingredients:

Plain (all-purpose) flour	300 g
Salt	1 tsp
Vegetable shortening	170 g
Cold water	4–6 Tbsp

Method:

- In a bowl, sift together the flour and salt. Add in the vegetable shortening and mix well using a fork. Slowly pour in the cold water a little at a time and mix into a dough.
- Shape the dough into balls, wrap in plastic sheet and set aside in the refrigerator for 1 hour before use.

CHEF'S NOTE: *A good alternative to the layered pastry is puff pastry. You can buy prepared puff pastry from the supermarket.*

Irish Brown Soda Bread

I got this recipe from Myrtle Allen, the chef and owner of Hotel Ballymaloe in Shanagarry, County Cork, Ireland. Mrs Allen is known worldwide for her traditional Irish cooking. In the original recipe for this soda bread, Mrs Allen used sour cream. I have changed it to yoghurt. I learnt from Mrs Allen that the bicarbonate of soda and the kneading technique are the two main factors that influence the texture of the bread. If too much bicarbonate of soda is used, the bread will taste a little bitter and its colour will be slightly dark. Too much kneading will make the bread rather heavy. Thus, the secret is to make sure that the dough is damp enough such that only a little kneading is necessary. Use your judgement. Happy trying!

Ingredients:

Attar flour (wholemeal flour)	600 g
Plain (all-purpose) flour	150 g, sifted
Oats	50 g
Bicarbonate of soda	1½ tsp
A pinch of salt	
Plain yoghurt	2 cups

Method:

- Preheat the oven to 250°C. Lightly grease the baking tray with butter.
- Mix together the attar, plain flour, oats, bicarbonate of soda and salt.
- Using a wooden spoon, beat the yoghurt before adding it to the flour mixture. If the resulting dough is too thick, add a little more yoghurt.
- Remove the dough from the bowl and knead gently on a floured surface for a short while. Divide the dough into 3 portions and shape into flat, round loaves. Use a knife and mark the top of each portion with a cross.
- Bake in the oven for 15 minutes. Then reduce the temperature to 200°C. Continue baking for another 15–20 minutes. Tap the bread to test if it is cooked. A hollow sound means it is done.

Mary Ryan's Chicken Pie

In England, pies are popularly served in pubs. They are also popular picnic meals. I still remember one summer in Ireland when my foster father, Neil and I went out for a walk. On the way, we visited Neil's cousin, Mary, who was at that time busy preparing chicken pies for her children. The aroma was so tempting! Fortunately for me, Mary had made some extra and I had my fill.

Ingredients:

Stock:
Chicken	1 (about 2 kg)
Carrot	1, peeled and quartered
Celery	1 stalk, thickly sliced
Onion	1, peeled and quartered
Thyme	1 tsp
Bay leaf	1
Parsley leaves	1 sprig, chopped

Filling:
Butter	100 g
Onion	1, peeled and cut into small cubes
Plain (all-purpose) flour	110 g, sifted
Carrot	1, peeled and cut into small cubes
Green peas	1/2 cup
Clear wine	5/8 cup
Thick cream	1 cup
Salt and ground white pepper to taste	
Button mushrooms	12, quartered

Pastry:
Ready-ti-use puff pastry	225 g
Egg yolk	1, beaten

Method:

Making the stock:
- Fill a pot with water to immerse the chicken. Add carrot, onion celery, thyme, bay leaf and chopped parsley. Simmer for 2 hours or until chicken is tender.
- Remove chicken and shred the meat. Put carcass back into stock. Boil and reduce to 4-cup quantity. Strain.

Making the filling:
- Heat a saucepan and melt the butter. Sauté onion and plain flour until almost golden brown. Add carrot, peas, wine and stock. Simmer until liquid is reduced by half. Stir in cream, chicken meat, salt and ground white pepper. Cook until sauce thickens. Add mushrooms. Transfer to a bowl to cool.

Preparing the pie:
- Preheat the over to 190°C.
- Roll out the pastry into a 1-cm thick sheet and cut rounds, according to the size of the pie moulds. Line the moulds with pastry and spoon in filling.
- Cut another piece of pastry to cover the top of the pie. Brush the edges with beaten egg yolk and use a fork to seal the edges. Brush the pie tops with beaten egg yolk. Make a 5-cm slit in the pastry cover to allow steam to escape during baking.
- Bake for 20 minutes until golden brown.

CHEF'S NOTE: *For those who do not take wine, substitute clear wine with prune juice.*

Pennequets Aux Fruits de Mer
(Seafood Pancake)

Crepes are very popular in France and they may be eaten with sweet or savoury fillings. There are various popular seafood dishes served with crepes in Brittany, southwest France, a place known for its beautiful beaches. The crepes served here are called *crepe bretonne*. A crepe is actually a very thin pancake and in Malaysia, some people associate it with *crepe suzette*, a dessert served with oranges. I first tried this seafood pancake at the Convention Market, near Montparnasse where I lived in Paris.

Ingredients:

Pancake:

Eggs	3
Milk	1¼ cups
Salt	½ tsp
Plain (all-purpose) flour	120 g, sifted
Butter	2 Tbsp, melted

Filling:

Butter for frying	
Shallots	3, peeled and finely chopped
Prawns (shrimps)	300 g, shelled, deveined and halved
White fish fillet	200 g, cut into small pieces
Fresh button mushrooms	200 g, thinly sliced
Fresh thyme	½ tsp
Clear wine	¼ cup
Prawn (shrimp) stock	2 cups
Crabmeat	200 g
Whipped cream	1 cup
Tomato puree	1 tsp
Parsley leaves	1 Tbsp, thinly sliced
Salt and ground white pepper to taste	
Spinach	100 g, blanched and drained
Parmesan cheese	50 g, grated
Gruyere cheese	50 g, grated

Method:

For the pancakes:

- Beat together eggs, milk and salt. Stir in flour and continue to beat, breaking up any lumps. Add butter and sieve batter into another bowl. Refrigerate for half hour before using.
- Heat a pan and grease lightly with butter. Pour 1 Tbsp batter to make a thin pancake. Cook until just golden brown and the sides begin to curl in. Transfer to a serving plate. Repeat until all the batter is used up.

For the filling:

- Heat butter and sauté shallots until almost soft. Add prawns, fish, mushrooms and thyme. Pour in wine and cook until slightly dry. Add stock, crabmeat, whipped cream, tomato puree and parsley. Cook until almost dry. Season with salt and ground white pepper.

To prepare the pancake:

- Preheat the oven to 180°C.
- Spread each pancake with the filling. Top with spinach leaves. Roll the pancake up and place on a baking tray. Repeat with all the pancakes. Any remaining filling may be poured over the pancake rolls and topped with grated cheese. Bake until the cheese melts and the pancakes are golden brown. Serve hot.

CHEF'S NOTE: *For those who do not take wine, the clear wine may be substituted with chicken stock.*

Poulet Rofi
(Grilled Chicken)

This dish is very popular in the remote district of France, particularly among farmers. I enjoy preparing this dish for dinner, especially when there are children around, as they love it.

Ingredients:

Free range chicken	1 (2.25 kg)
Butter	150 g
Paprika	1 Tsbp
Ground fennel	1 tsp
Fresh rosemary	1 tsp, chopped
Fresh thyme	1 tsp, chopped
Garlic	2 cloves, peeled and finely pounded
Lemon juice	extracted from 1 lemon
Salt	1 tsp
Ground black pepper	1 tsp
Groundnut oil for deep-frying	
Chicken bone stock or white wine	2 cups
Plain (all-purpose) flour	1 Tbsp
Salt and ground white pepper to taste	
Parsley leaves	1 Tbsp, chopped

Method:

- Preheat oven at 190°C.
- Clean the chicken and dry with kitchen towel. Keep aside.
- Mix together butter, paprika, fennel, resemary, thyme, garlic, lemon juice, salt and ground black pepper in a bowl. Stir until mixture is well blended.
- Slowly insert your finger under chicken skin to loosen the skin. Be careful that the skin does not tear. Continue until you have worked through the whole chicken.
- Spread the butter mixture underneath the skin of the whole chicken with your finger.
- Spread the remaining butter mixture on the surface of the chicken, Bind the feet with a string and tuck in the wings.
- Heat the groundnut oil in a wok and fry the chicken for a few minutes until golden brown, periodically turning the chicken over. Transfer chicken to a baking tray and cook in the oven for 45 minutes.
- When cooked, remove the chicken from the tray and wrap it with aluminium foil.
- Place the baking tray over low heat an allow the chicken juice to simmer. Meanwhile, take a spoonful of chicken juice and set aside.
- Add chicken stock or clear wine to enhance the taste of the sauce, stirring it in with the chicken juice in the tray. Remove from the heat.
- In a small saucepan, heat the spoonful of chicken juice and fry with plain flour until golden. Add the stock from the baking tray. Stir in a pinch of salt, black pepper and parsley leaves.
- Pour the sauce ove the grilled chicken to serve.

CHEF'S NOTE: *Grilled (Broiled) chicken tastes better if it is first fried in hot oil and then grilled in the oven. Frying the chicken first will cook the skin and prevent the juices from flowing out before the whole chicken is tender. To ensure that the chicken is cooked, prick the thickest part of the thigh with a fork. The juice that flows out should be clear, not reddish in colour. If you are using a beef thermometer, place the thermometer on the thickest ar of the thigh. The temperature should be 90°C.*

Grillade de Beef, Marchand de Vin
(Grilled Beef with Butter)

The secret of preparing good steak lies in the quality of the beef, the way it is cooked and the suitability of the sauce. Good quality beef is usually dark pink in colour and has less fat. The fillet is the softest and most expensive part but it does not taste as good the flank and skirt. The sirloin or New York parts make very good steaks. Steaks can be grilled on a heavy-bottom pan or on glowing charcoal. But remember that the soft parts of the meat will cook faster than the tough parts. Before grilling, thaw the frozen meat for at least one hour. Good quality meat will not taste as good if it is simply mixed with spices and herbs and left aside. Instead, sprinkle some salt and freshly ground black pepper on the meat and rub it with some olive oil before grilling. Do not rub salt into the beef too long before grilling as this will dry out the meat.

This grilled (broiled) beef recipe is a traditional one and is commonly used in French restaurants in Paris. A good red wine will enhance the taste of the butter sauce.

Ingredients:

Sirloin steak	4 slices (200 g per piece)
Black peppercorns	1 Tbsp, finely ground
Salt to taste	
Olive oil	

Marchand de Vin Butter Sauce:

Fine red wine	³/₄ cup
Shallots	1 Tbsp, peeled and finely chopped
Beef stock	4 Tbsp
Unsalted butter	170 g, softened
Lemon juice	1 Tbsp
Parsley leaves	1 Tbsp, chopped
Salt and ground black pepper to taste	

Method:

For the butter sauce:

- Bring to the boil red wine and shallots until the wine is reduced to a ¹/₃-cup quantity. Set aside to cool.
- Mix the red wine with the other ingredients and beat until well-combined. Place on greaseproof paper and roll up like a cigarette. Refrigerate for a few hours.

For the steak:

- Heat the olive oil in a saucepan and pan-fry or grill the steak until cooked. Transfer to a plate and serve with potato chips and vegetables.
- Cut two pieces of the hardened butter sauce and place on the steak. The butter will melt and form the sauce for the steak. Serve hot.

CHEF'S NOTE: *For those who do not take wine, the red wine may be substituted with prune juice.*

Quiche Aux Fruits de Mer
(Seafood Quiche)

The first time I tried making this recipe was in the kitchen of the Ritz Hotel in Paris. At the Ritz, everything is done with care and in great detail, resulting in high quality food that is always delicious. This quiche is one of the best I have ever tasted. Serve it for lunch or as an afternoon teatime treat!

Ingredients:

Pastry:

Plain (all-purpose) flour	250 g, sifted
A pinch of salt	
Butter	170 g, chilled and cut into small pieces
Egg	1, lightly beaten
Water, if required	

Filling:

Butter for sautéing	
Shallots	1 Tbsp, finely chopped
Red snapper fillet	100 g, cut into pieces
Prawn (shrimps) meat	100 g
Crab meat	200 g
Salt and ground white pepper to taste	

Custard:

Eggs	2
Egg yolks	4
Fresh milk	1 cup
Thick cream	1 cup
Curry powder	1/2 tsp

Garnish:

Parsley leaves	1 Tbsp, chopped

Method:

For the pastry:

- Combine the flour and salt and rub in the butter quickly until the mixture resembles breadcrumbs. Add egg and blend well. If necessary, add water to make a soft dough.
- Shape the dough into a ball and wrap with plastic sheet. Refrigerate for 30 minutes.
- Roll out the dough into a 1 cm-thick sheet and press it into a 25-cm greased quiche tin. Bake in the oven at 180°C for 15 minutes.

For the filling:

- In a pan, heat the butter and sauté the shallots until golden brown. Put in fish, prawns and crabmeat. Add salt and ground white pepper. Allow to cool.

For the custard:

- Beat together the eggs, egg yolks, fresh milk, thick cream and curry powder. Strain.

Preparing the quiche:

- Preheat the oven to 170°C.
- Put the filling into the prepared pastry.
- Pour the custard on top of the filling. Sprinkle with parsley.
- Bake for 25–30 minutes until the filling is cooked and golden brown. Serve hot.

CHEF'S NOTE: *Avoid kneading the dough for too long. Dough that is kneaded quickly and chilled will make a crisp pastry. Roll the dough out between two sheets of plastic or greased baking paper for easy handling.*

Bouillabaisse
(Fish Soup from the South of France)

This dish is served traditionally with toasted garlic bread, grated Gruyere cheese and *rouille*. *Rouille* is a sauce made from ground chilli, pounded garlic and olive oil. Almost all the restaurants along the French Riviera have their own ways of preparing the Bouillabaisse. The name is derived from the methods employed in cooking the dish: *bouille* which means boiling and *baisse* which means lowering the temperature. The original Bouillabaisse is usually prepared from eight to ten types of fish found in the Mediterranean sea. You can also use the hardtail, grouper, threadfin and mackerel. Below is the Bouillabaisse ala Malaysia, my own creation!

Ingredients:

Fish stock:

Olive oil	3/4 cup
Onions	2, peeled and finely chopped
Garlic	2 cloves, peeled and finely chopped
Fish bones	1 kg (including the head)
Ripe tomatoes	6, seeded and thinly sliced
Fresh rosemary	3 sprigs, chopped
Fresh thyme	2 sprigs, chopped
Bay leaf	1
Water	16 cups
Saffron strands	1 tsp
Ground dried chillies	1 tsp

Soup:

Olive oil	1 Tbsp
Potatoes	4, peeled and thinly sliced
Fish fillet	2 kg (of fish mentioned above), cut into pieces
Prawns (shrimps) meat	300 g
Salt and ground white pepper to taste	

Method:

- In a pot large enough to hold 16 cups of water, heat the olive oil and stir-fry the onions, garlic and fish bones for a few minutes. Add the tomatoes and fresh rosemary, thyme and bay leaf. Cook until fragrant. Pour in water and add the saffron strands and ground dried chillies. Cook for 20 minutes. Strain the fish stock with a muslin cloth.
- To prepare the Bouillabaisse, heat the olive oil in a pan and fry the potatoes until soft.
- Mix together the fish, prawns and fish stock. Bring to the boil. Add salt and ground white pepper to taste. Serve hot.

CHEF'S NOTE: *For a richer fish stock, add in as many bones and fish heads as possible.*

Les Farcis (Stuffed Vegetables)

Le Farcis or stuffed vegetables are very popular in the Mediterranean. In southern France, you can have them at most restaurants and delis. Several types of vegetables may be used including the purple aubergines (eggplants), courgettes (zucchinis), tomatoes and onions. Scoop out the flesh of the vegetables and fill it with minced meat, grated cheese, herbs and spices. Then grill (broil) them.

I still remember the small restaurant I dined at in Nice. It was called the Vieille Ville. The wide array of stuffed vegetables on display prompted me to have my dinner there. The food was so delicious that I will never forget the restaurant. This is my version of Les Fracis.

Ingredients:

Zucchinis (Courgettes)	2, cut into 6 pieces
Onions	3 medium, peeled
Salt to taste	
Long aubergines (eggplants)	2, cut into 6 pieces
Tomatoes	4 medium

Filling:

Oilve oil for trying	
Minced beef	250 g
Onion	1, peeled and finely chopped
Garlic	2 cloves, peeled and finely chopped
Parsley leaves	1 sprig, chopped
Cooked rice	6 Tbsp
Salt and ground black pepper to taste	
Parmesan cheese	2 Tbsp, grated
Egg	1, beaten

Method:

- Preheat the oven to 190°C.
- In a pot of water, boil the zucchinis and onions for 1 minute. Add a pinch of salt. Remove from heat and scoop out the flesh. Scoop out the aubergines and tomatoes into a bowl. Set aside.
- Heat a saucepan with olive oil and stir-fry the minced beef with onion. Add the vegetable flesh and fry for a short while. Mix in the parsley leaves, cooked rice, salt, ground black pepper, cheese and egg.
- Stuff the ingredients into the vegetable skins. Grease a baking tray with olive oil and arrange the stuffed vegetables on it. Brush the tops with a little butter and bake for half hour.

CHEF'S NOTE: *Cabbage leaves may be used as an alternative to the vegetable skins. They should be blanched and used to wrap the filling before baking. In French, this cabbage dish is known as Capounets.*

La Vraie Pissaladiere
(Onions, Olives and Anchovies Tart)

The Spanish love eating olives and it's no wonder that olives are commonly used in Spanish kitchens. Olives are also the main snack in many tapas bars or cafés in Spain. It is used in salads, egg dishes, stews and sauces. This is of my favourite savoury tarts. try it for yourself!

Ingredients:

Tart base:

Instant yeast	1 Tbsp
Honey	1 tsp
Warm water	1½ cups
Bread flour	450 g, sifted
Salt	1 tsp
Olive oil	3 Tbsp

Filling:

Olive oil for frying	
Yellow onions	1.5 kg, peeled and thinly sliced
Garlic	2 cloves, peeled and finely chopped
Mixed herbs (fresh thyme, rosemary and basil)	1 Tbsp, chopped
Salt and ground black pepper	
Pickled anchovies	6
Black olives	30 g (at least 11 olives)

Method:

For the tart base:

- Preheat the oven to 180°C.
- Blend the instant yeast, honey and warm water in an electric mixer, using a bread dough hook. Beat at a slow speed for 5 minutes. Add bread flour, salt and olive oil and knead for another 5 minutes.
- Divide the dough into 4 portions and shape into balls. Leave the dough in the mixing bowl, cover with a damp cloth and leave for 1½ hours until the dough rises to twice its original size.
- Roll out each portion into 2.5-cm-thick rounds and place on a greased baking tray.
- In a pan, heat the oilive oil and fry the onions until golden brown. Add garlic, mixed herbs, salt and ground black pepper to taste.
- Spread the onion mixture on the prepared dough and top with pickled anchovies and olives. Bake for half hour until the bread base is almost crisp. Serve hot.

Epaule d'agneau Farcie Provencale
(Provencale Lamb Shoulder)

Ingredients:

Lamb shoulder	2.25 kg, cut into 2, meat loosened from bones

Filling:

Breadcrumbs	200 g
Parsley leaves	2 tsp, chopped
Fresh tarragon	2 tsp
Fresh chervil	2 tsp
Garlic	2–3 cloves, peeled and finely chopped
Eggs	2, beaten
Salt and ground white pepper to taste	
Black olives	60 g, pitted
Butter	100 g
Carrots	5, peeled and sliced
Tomatoes	3, thickly sliced
Onion	1, peeled and chopped
Celery	1 stalk, chopped
Clear dry wine	1 cup
Fresh parsley leaves	1 tsp, chopped
Bay leaf	1
Fresh tyhme	1 tsp
Ground black pepper to taste	

Method:
- Preheat the oven to 220°C.
- To make the filling, combine breadcrumbs, parsley, tarragon, chervil, garlic and eggs in a bowl. Season with salt and ground white pepper.
- Spread the filling on the lamb, arrange the black olives in the middle and roll the meat up tightly. Secure neatly with a string.
- Melt 60 g butter in a saucepan and fry the lamb until almost golden. Add carrots, tomatoes, onion and celery. Stir-fry for 2 minutes. Pour in the clear wine, add in parsley, bay leaf and fresh thyme, salt and ground black pepper. Bring to the boil.
- Transfer the lamb, vegetables and sauce to a baking tray and bake for about 1 hour. Occasionally, scoop the sauce from the baking tray and pour over the lamb to wet it.
- When the lamb is cooked, remove from the baking tray. Pour out the oil from the baking tray into a saucepan and bring to the boil over low heat until it thickens. Strain the oil. Use this as sauce for the lamb.

CHEF'S NOTE: *For those who do not take wine, clear wine may be substituted with chicken stock.*

Gratin Dauphinoise
(Baked Layered Potato)

The French are very creative in cooking potatoes. They boil, steam, grill (broil) or simply fry it. This classic French potato dish is commonly made at home parties. It tastes delicious especially when served with a meat or chicken dish. Traditionally, the potatoes are cut thinly, about the width of a coin. You may use Idaho potatoes. Wash the potatoes before they are cut (instead of after) to preserve the taste when cooked.

Ingredients:

Garlic	2 cloves, peeled
Potatoes	1 kg, peeled and thinly sliced
Gruyere cheese	100 g
Fresh milk	2 cups
Thick cream	1/2 cup
Ground black pepper to taste	
Salt	1 tsp
Ground nutmeg	1/2 tsp
Butter	4 Tbsp

Method:
- Preheat the oven to 190°C.
- Bruise the garlic and spread on a 35 x 23 x 5-cm baking tray. Arrange the potato slices in layers on the tray to resemble fish scales. Sprinkle cheese on top. Repeat laying potato slices and sprinkling cheese until all the potato slices are used up.
- In another bowl, mix the fresh milk, thick cream, ground black pepper, salt and nutmeg. Pour the mixture onto the potatoes on the baking tray. Drop the butter on top of the mixture and bake in the oven for 45 minutes until dry and the potatoes are golden brown. Serve hot.

Curried Chicken and Mango Salad

Curry powder is an important ingredient in various Caribbean recipes. This is one such recipe. You may use any type of curry powder, but I would recommend original Caribbean curry powder for a truly authentic flavour. I have included two curry powder recipes here—Jamaican and Trinidad. You may use either one. Like curry powder, mango is a popular ingredient in Caribbean cooking. A combination of the two would certainly not disappoint you. This recipe is very simple: Prepare a sauce and mix it with the chicken and mango, then cool before serving. You may use pineapple as an alternative to mango, or you can even use both. This dish works well as an appetiser especially when you're having a barbecue.

While on holiday in Jamaica, I was fascinated by the way the locals ate their mangoes. They pick a ripe mango and rub it until it is soft. They then cut off one end of the mango and suck the juice and the fibre out. Now, whenever I don't feel like peeling mangoes, I will eat it like the Jamaicans. So don't be shocked if you see me walking in the market and sipping mango juice from a whole ripe mango!

Ingredients:

Chicken breast	4 pieces (about 300g)
Salt	1 tsp
Ground white pepper	1 tsp

Sauce:

Mayonnaise	1 cup
Tabasco sauce	1 tsp
Caribbean curry powder*	3 tsp
Garlic	2 cloves, peeled and finely chopped
Spring onions (Scallions)	3, finely sliced
Parsley leaves	2 Tbsps, chopped
Mango flesh	60 g, pureed
Ground black pepper	1 tsp
Sweet mangoes	2, peeled, stone and cut into small cubes

Method:

- Preheat the oven to 180°C.
- Season chicken with salt and ground white pepper. Grill (broil) for 10 minutes. Refrigerate for a few hours before cutting the meat into small cubes.
- To make the sauce, mix the mayonnaise, Tabasco sauce, curry powder, garlic, spring onions, parsley, mango puree, salt and ground black pepper until well combined.
- In a separate bowl, mix the mango and chicken cubes. Add the sauce and mix well. Refrigerate salad for 2 hours to allow it to mature. Serve.

* Trinidad Curry Powder :

Ingredients (Mix together):

Ground star anise	1 1/2 tsp
Poppy seeds	1 1/2 tsp
Ground black pepper	1 1/2 tsp
Ground coriander	1 Tbsp
Ground cumin	1 Tbsp
Chilli powder	1 Tbsp
Ground cinnamon	1 Tbsp
Ground turmeric	6 Tbsp
Ground ginger	4 Tbsp

** Jamaican Curry Powder :

Ingredients (Mix together):

Ground coriander	55 g
Ground turmeric	55 g
Ground black pepper	55 g
Ground ginger	55 g
Ground fenugreek	2 Tbsp
Ground cinnamon	2 Tbsp

Fish Soup

In the Caribbean Islands, there are many varieties of soup and all are heavy and thick. Many ingredients are added into a bowl of soup and it is difficult to see what you are eating. I asked a chef in Haiti why their soups are so heavy and rich, and he explained to me that soup was originally the humble food of the slaves. As it was all they had to eat after a hard day's work, they put whatever ingredients they had into it to make a good meal. Today, soup is still a staple diet among the villagers in the rural areas.

I tasted several types of soups while in the Caribbean, but none was as mouthwatering as the fish soup I sampled in a restaurant in Puerto Rico. This soup bears the characteristics of Spanish cooking as Puerto Rico was once under Spanish rule. In Italy, this soup is known as *cioppino*. Although this recipe uses fish, you may substitute it with other seafood.

Ingredients:

Olive oil	1/2 cup
Onions	2, peeled and cut into small cubes
Garlic	2 cloves, peeled and finely chopped
Carrot	1, peeled and finely sliced
Leek	2 stalks, sliced
Tomatoes	2, thinly sliced
Fish stock	3 cups
Bay leaf	1
Red snapper meat	200 g, sliced
Clear wine	1 cup
Lime juice	extracted from 1 lime
Prawns (shrimps)	300 g, shelled and deveined
Red capsicum (bell pepper)	1/2, cut into small cubes
A pinch of cayenne pepper	
Squid	200 g, cleaned and sliced
A pinch of salt	
Parsley leaves	1 sprig, finely chopped for garnishing

Method:

- In a pan, heat some olive oil and sauté the onions, garlic, carrots and leeks until soft. Add the tomatoes, fish stock, bay leaf and red snapper meat. Simmer for 20 minutes. Pour in the clear wine and lime juice. Add in the prawns, capsicums, cayenne pepper, squid and salt. Cook for another 10 minutes.
- Transfer to a serving bowl and sprinkle parsley leaves over. Serve hot with a crusty loaf.

Coconut Prawn Fritters

A combination of crispy prawns (shrimps), coconut and eight types of spices makes this an excellent entrée. In the Caribbean, besides prawns, fish is also a very popular cooking ingredient. In the Dominican Republic, smaller fish called *ti ti-oui*, which look like the mackerel found in Malaysia, is prepared in the same way as the prawns in this recipe. As the fish is small, it is usually prepared whole.

Ingredients:

Ground coriander	2 tsp
Paprika	1½ tsp
Ground black pepper	1½ tsp
Salt	2 tsp
Onion powder	1¾ tsp
Garlic powder	1 tsp
Fresh oregano	2 tsp
Fresh thyme	2 tsp
Ground cayenne pepper	1 Tbsp
Beer	1 can (375 ml)
Plain (all-purpose) flour	265 g, sifted
Baking soda	1 Tbsp
Prawns (shrimps)	1 kg (about 50 medium), shelled and deveined
Desiccated coconut	270 g
Cooking oil for frying	

Method:

- In a bowl, mix together ground coriander, paprika, ground black pepper, salt, onion and, garlic powder, fresh oregano and thyme and ground cayenne pepper.
- In another bowl, combine the beer, plain flour and baking soda. Add the mixed spices and stir well. Dip the prawns in the batter and coat with desiccated coconut.
- Fry prawns in hot cooking oil until golden brown. Drain on absorbent peper. Serve with lettuce leaves and chilli sauce.)

CHEF'S NOTE: *The beer used in this recipe may be substituted with water and juice from ¼ lemon.*

Tropical Barbecue Prawns

This lovely dish is usually served with paratha or naan. You may also use it as a sandwich filling. As a variation to the recipe, you may replace the prawns (shrimps) with fish or crabmeat. Whichever meat you choose, this dish is truly sensational!

Ingredients:

Large prawns (shrimps)	2 kg, shelled and deveined
Onion	1, peeled and cut into big cubes
Capsicum (bell pepper)	1, cut into big cubes
Limes	2, each cut in half

Marinade:

Oranges juice	extracted from 3 oranges
Garlic	3 cloves, peeled and pounded into a paste
Spring onions (scallions)	2, finely sliced
Worcestershire sauce	1/4 cup

Barbecue Sauce:

Vegetable oil	1/4 cup
Demerara	55 g
Garlic	3 cloves, peeled and pounded into a fine paste
Onion	1, peeled and cut into small cubes
Ground fennel	2 Tbsp
Shallot	1, peeled and pounded into a fine paste
Orange	1, peeled and finely sliced
Tomatoes	3, coarsely blended
Tomato sauce	1 cup
Lemon juice	extracted from 2 lemons
Ground black pepper	1 Tbsp
Ground cayenne pepper	1 tsp
Ground white pepper	2 Tbsp
A dash of Tabasco sauce	

Method:

- Combine the ingredients for the marinade in a bowl. Put prawns in. Refrigerate for 1 hour.
- To make the barbecue sauce, heat the vegetable oil in a pot and add the demerara, stirring constantly over medium heat until it caramelises. Add the garlic and onion and fry until soft. Stir in the ground fennel and shallots. Add the oranges and blended tomato. Cook for another 10 minutes and add the tomato sauce, lemon juice and marinated prawns.
- Cook until the gravy is slightly thick before adding in the ground black pepper, ground cayenne pepper, ground white pepper and Tabasco sauce. Add sugar to sweeten the barbecue sauce if desired.
- On a skewer, alternate a prawn, onion cube, capsicum cube and lime segment. Grill (broil) over glowing charcoal, basting the prawns with barbecue sauce occasionally. Serve hot with the barbecue sauce.

Mango Pepper Pot

This sauce is frequently served as a dip with grilled (broiled) chicken. It is similar to the raw pickles we have in Malaysia.

Ingredients:

Ripe mangoes	3, peeled and cut into small cubes
Onion	1, peeled and cut into small cubes
Green chillies	2, finely sliced
Vinegar	1/4 cup
Olive oil	1/4 cup
Salt and ground white pepper to taste	
Coriander leaves (cilantro)	2 Tbsp, finely chopped

Method:
- Mix all the ingredients together and set aside for 1 hour before serving.

Red Pepper Remoulade

Ingredients:

Red chilli	1, finely chopped
Paprika	1 Tbsp
Salt	1 tsp
Sugar and ground white pepper to taste	
Parsley leaves	3 Tbsp, finely chopped
Tomato sauce	3 Tbsp
Garlic	2 cloves, peeled and finely chopped
Dijon mustard	2 Tbsp
Mayonnaise	1 cup

Method:
- Combine all ingredients in a bowl and leave to marinate overnight before serving.

Clockwise from top: Mango Pepper Pot, Avocado Sauce, Pickled Onion (*recipe on page 158*), Pineapple Vinaigrette, Salsa Naranja, Red Pepper Remoulade, and Mango Chutney *(centre)*.

Pineapple Vinaigrette

Pineapples grow well in the Caribbean Islands, especially on the volcanic islands where the acidic soil favours their growth. This delightful sauce originates from the Caribbean and is enjoyed with seafood salads or grilled (broiled) fish and squid.

Ingredients:

Coriander leaves (cilantro)	1 Tbsp, chopped
Olive oil	3/4 cup
Lime juice	extracted from 1 lime
Vinegar	1/3 cup
Concentrated pineapple juice	1/4 cup
Garlic	2 cloves, peeled and finely chopped
Dijon mustard	2 Tbsp
Salt and ground white pepper to taste	

Method:
- Combine all the ingredients in a blender and blend into a fine paste. Serve as a dip or salad dressing.

Salsa Naranja

This is similar to the raw pineapple, cucumber and onion salad served in Malaysia. In Jamaica, Salsa Naranja is served with samosas or *empanadas*, a curry puff-like snack made with parkoras.

Ingredients:

Sugar	110 g
Water	1 cup
Oranges	2, peeled and diced
Pineapple	1/2, peeled and diced
Fresh orange juice	1 cup
Black rum	2 Tbsp
Corn flour (cornstarch)	2 tsp, blended with a little water

Method:
- Bring to the boil the sugar and water until the syrup is almost thick. Add oranges, pineapple, orange juice and rum and cook for 10 minutes. Stir in corn flour and simmer until the sauce is thick. Set aside to cool before serving.

Mango Chutney

This chutney goes well with curry dishes. It is also eaten with barbecued food in most of the Caribbean.

Ingredients:

Unripe mango	800g, peeled and diced
Sultanas (raisins)	150 g
Preserved dates	300 g
Ginger	100 g, peeled and pounded into a fine paste
Garlic	4 cloves, peeled
Demerara sugar	400 g
Mustard seeds	2 tsp
Green and red chillies	3, sliced
Onions	2, peeled and diced
Salt and ground white pepper to taste	
Ground turmeric	1 tsp
Vinegar	½ cup

Method:

- Cook all the ingredients over medium heat for 45 minutes until the mixture thickens. Cool before serving.

CHEF'S NOTE: *If you prefer the chutney to be more sour, add more vinegar.*

Avocado Sauce

Among the various sauces served with seafood in the Caribbean, this is definitely my favourite. It is also an excellent accompaniment to grilled (broiled) beef or chicken and can also be used as a sandwich spread.

Ingredients:

Ripe avocado	5, stoned, peeled and cut into small pieces
Lime juice	2 cups
Onion	1, peeled
Coriander leaves (cilantro)	1 sprig
Parsley leaves	1 Tbsp, chopped
Garlic	1 clove, peeled and chopped
Salt and ground white pepper to taste	
Stuffed olives	45 g
Green capsicums (bell peppers)	1, chopped
Capers	2 Tbsp
White wine	½ cup
Orange juice	½ cup
A dash of Tobasco sauce	

Method:

- Blend the acovados, lime juice, onion, capsicum, coriander leaves, parsley, garlic, salt ground white pepper, olives and capers into fine paste in a blender. Add in the remaining ingredients and mix well.

CHEF'S NOTE: *White wine can be substituted with stock.*

Barbados-style Fried Fish

The first time I tasted this fish was when I was out sightseeing in the Barbados islands. Every Friday and Saturday night, there would be night market set up along Baxter Road and a wide variety of local delicacies would be on sale. I enjoy patronising such stalls whenever I am overseas, as it allows me to sample all the local delights. The aroma of the fried fish was what attracted me and then I saw a long queue of people at the stall. After tasting the fish, I understood why it was so popular! The next evening, I asked the stallholder to share his recipe with me and he did. My principle in life is to ask and you will be answered—but don't forget to flash your wide smile!

Ingredients

Spring onion (scallion)	1, finely chopped
Capsicum (bell pepper)	1, cut into fine strips
Onion	1, peeled and chopped
Garlic	4 cloves, peeled and chopped
Coriander leaves (cilantro)	5 sprigs
Fresh marjoram	2 Tbsp
Fresh thyme	2 Tbsp
Lime juice,	extracted from 2 limes
Red snapper or grouper fillet	6 slices (200 g per slice)
Salt	1 tsp
Ground black pepper	1 tsp
Ground chilli	1 tsp
Egg	1, beaten
Breadcrumbs	400 g
Cooking oil for frying	

Method:

- Blend the spring onion, capsicum, onion, garlic, coriander, marjoram, thyme, and lime juice into a paste.
- Season the fish fillets with salt, ground black pepper, ground chilli and some of the blended paste. If the fillet is thick, slit the sides and stuff the paste into the slits.
- Dip the fish in egg and coat with breadcrumbs. Fry with a little cooking oil over medium heat until golden brown on both sides. Serve with lime slices and Pickled Onions*.

*Pickled Onions

Ingredients:

Spanish onions	3, peeled
Vinegar	1 cup
Castor sugar	1 tsp
Black peppercorns	3, freshly cracked
Green chilli	1, diced

Method:

- Combine all the ingredients in a bowl and leave to marinate for 2 days before serving.

Pan Fried Grouper with Creole Sauce

My first taste of this delicious dish was at one of the restaurants in Barbados. A popular tourist destination, Barbados is also known for the many large sugarcane plantations on the island. Every year, when the harvest season is over, there will be a huge celebration which will last for a month. Various cultural activities will be held, including a dance competition backed by the world-famous calypso music.

Ingredients:

Grouper fillet	4 slices (200 g per slice)
Lime juice	1 cup
Plain (all-purpose) flour to coat the fish	
Cooking oil for frying	

Creole Sauce:

Olive oil	1/4 cup
Green chillies	2, finely sliced
Onion	1, peeled and chopped
Tomato sauce	1 can (225 g)
Clear wine	1/2 cup
Ground black pepper	1 tsp
Fresh thyme	1 tsp
Basil leaf	1 tsp, chopped
Salt	1/2 tsp

Method:

For the fish:

- Marinate the fish in lime juice for 1 hour. Do not leave it too long, as the flesh will break up.
- Remove the fish from the lime juice and pat dry with a paper towel. Roll the fish in plain flour and fry with little cooking oil, turning the fish over occasionally until both sides are evenly browned. Serve the fish with Creole sauce.

For the sauce:

- Heat the olive oil, and sauté the green chillies and onion until soft. Add the tomato sauce, clear wine, ground black pepper, fresh thyme and basil leaves and salt. Allow the sauce to thicken and simmer for 15 minutes.

Island Paradise Crabcakes

I tried this dish was while I was onboard a yacht named *Island Paradise*—that's why I've named the crabscakes after it. We were on a diving trip in the waters around St. Lucia Island. It was my first diving experience and our guide, Jean Pierrier, a Frenchman, brought us to observe the beautiful marine life. For lunch, Jean's wife, Biba, a Jamaican, prepared several delicious salads and sandwiches for us. In my sandwich was a crabcake.

To me, St. Lucia island, is the most beautiful island in the Caribbean. Its forest, mountain ranges and the birds add to the exoticness of this island. There are also several extinct volcanoes, but I was still rather nervous when we were at the foot of one of the volcanoes.

An annual flower festival, *La Rose, La Marguerite,* is one of the major attractions on St. Lucia Island. During this festival, many beautifully decorated floats parade the streets, accompanied by the samba dancers and calypso music.

Ingredients:

Prawns (shrimps)	200 g, shelled and deveined, finely chopped
Crabmeat	500 g
Green chilli	2, finely sliced
Garlic	4 cloves, peeled and finely chopped
Mayonnaise	2 Tbsp
Tomatoes	2, seeded and cut into small pieces
Onion	1/2, finely chopped
Coriander leaves (cilantro)	1 sprig, finely sliced
Salt	1/2 tsp
Ground white pepper	1/2 tsp
Breadcrumbs	100 g
Cooking oil for frying	

Method:

- In a bowl, combine all the ingredient, except cooking oil, and shape to form a patty 7.5 cm in diameter.
- Heat some cooking oil in a pan and fry the patties until golden brown on both sides. Serve as a snack on its own or as a sandwich filling.

Crab Pilau

Among the many islands of the Caribbean, Trinidad and Tobago are the most populated and diverse in ethnicity. The people migrated from Africa, the Middle East and China, and there are also people of French, Portuguese, English and Indian descent. Due to their multi-ethnicity and multicultural backgrounds, the way food is prepared on these islands varies in style. I obtained this Crab Pilau recipe from an Indian-Caribbean restaurant on the island.

Ingredients:

Crabmeat	300 g
Ground black pepper	1 tsp
Salt	1 tsp
Lime juice	extracted from 1 lime
Butter	115 g
Onion	1, peeled and diced
Garlic	2 cloves, peeled and finely chopped
Green chilli	1, finely sliced
Meat curry powder	2 Tbsp
Tomato	1, diced
Basmati rice	350 g
Coconut milk	3$\frac{1}{2}$ cups

Method:
- Season the crabmeat with ground black pepper, salt and lime juice. Refrigerate for 1 hour.
- In a pot, melt the butter and sauté the onion, garlic and green chilli until soft. Add the curry powder and stir-fry for another few minutes. Stir in the tomato and fry for another few minutes. Add the rice, stirring continuously, and pour in the coconut milk. Add salt and cook until the mixture is almost dry. Stir in the marinated crabmeat and cook for 5 minutes more before taking off the heat. Serve hot.

Stuffed Paw-paw

Papayas are known as paw-paw in the Caribbean. The fruit is used in soups, cocktail drinks and salads. The first time I tasted this Stuffed Paw-paw dish was at the annual Pirate Week Festival in Caymen Island. It is believed that there once lived a fearsome pirate named Blackbeard whose ship sank in the waters off this island. Blackbeard managed to rescue his treasure and buried it on the island. Hundreds of years later, the people on the island began celebrating the legend in the form of a week-long festival. Throughout the week of festivities, they would don pirate or sailor costumes and hunt for Blackbeard's treasure. I took part in the hunt, hoping to leave the island a millionaire. Alas, luck was not with me!

Ingredients:

Paw-paw (papaya)	2 small, almost ripe
Butter	60 g
Onion	1, peeled and diced
Shallot	1, peeled and finely chopped
Carrot	1, peeled and cut into small cubes
Capsicum (bell pepper)	1, cut into small cubes
Tomato	1, diced
Crabmeat	600 g
Coriander leaves (cilantro)	1/2 sprig, finely chopped
Salt	1/2 tsp
Fresh thyme	1/2 tsp
Fresh oregano	1/2 tsp
Clear wine	1/2 cup
Brandy	1 Tbsp
Breadcrumbs	50 g
Ground white and black pepper to taste	

Method:

- Preheat the oven to 180°C.
- Cut each paw-paw in half and scoop out the flesh. Cut the flesh into cubes. Set the paw-paw shells and flesh aside.
- Heat a pan and melt the butter. Sauté the onion, shallot, carrot, capsicum, tomato and paw-paw cubes. Add the crabmeat, coriander leaves, salt, fresh thyme and oregano. Pour in the clear wine and brandy. Bring to the boil for 5 minutes.
- Add the breadcrumbs and stir in white and black pepper. When well-combined, scoop the filling into the paw-paw shells and bake for 30 minutes.

CHEF'S NOTE: *In this recipe, brandy may be substituted with prune juice and clear wine with chicken stock.*

Cod Fish with Coconut

Cod fish or *bacalao*, as it is known in Spanish, can be prepared in many ways, but the best method is to steam it. If cod fish is not available, you may use dried threadfin in this recipe. All you have to do is soak the dried threadfin overnight, boil it for 10 minutes and drain the water so that it would not be too salty. This recipe originated from the Dominican Republic where coconut is commonly used in stews, soups and desserts.

Ingredients:

Olive oil	1/4 cup
Green chilli	1, finely sliced
Onion	1, peeled and finely chopped
Garlic	2 cloves, peeled and finely chopped
Tomatoes	2, diced
Thick coconut milk	1 cup
Dried threadfin fillet	600 g, diced
Parsley	2 Tbsp chopped
Coriander leaves (cilantro)	2 Tbsp, finely chopped
Water	1/2 cup
Potatoes	2, peeled and cut into small cubes
Red chilli	1, pounded into a fine paste
Ground black pepper	1 tsp
Grated young coconut	100 g
Salt	1 tsp

Method:

- Heat the olive oil in a pan and sauté the green chilli, onion and garlic until soft. Add the tomatoes and thick coconut milk and bring to the boil for 5 minutes.
- Stir in the threadfin, parsley and coriander leaves, water, potatoes, red chillies, black pepper and grated coconut. Season with salt. Cook until the mixture thickens.
- Garnish with chopped coriander leaves and serve hot with white rice.

Poulet Fricasse Gaudeloupe

I acquired this Caribbean recipe several years ago from a New York food magazine that featured famous restaurants in the West Indies. After several attempts, I perfected the recipe and I now enjoy serving it to guests for dinner.

Original Caribbean cuisine is hard to come by even in the Caribbean islands. Most hotels and restaurants serve meals that cater to what their guests are used to and thus many tourists never get to taste the original cuisine of the Caribbean.

In Gaudeloupe, however, several restaurants serving original Caribbean cuisine can be found along the beaches. In mid-August every year, the tourism office in Gaudeloupe organises a Chef Festival where chefs (about 200, mostly women) will don their traditional costumes complete with interesting head gear and fine jewellery. They will carry decorative baskets filled with the island's best produce and parade along the road towards the hall where the cooking festival will be held. Along the way, the chefs will dance to the rhythm of the samba and inadvertedly, some of the contents in their baskets will fall out. I find the whole process very entertaining.

Ingredients:

Chicken	1 (1.5 kg), cut into 12 pieces
Lime juice	3/4 cup
Ground black pepper	1 Tbsp
Fine salt	1 Tbsp
Spring onions (scallions)	3–4, chopped
Parsley leaves	1 sprig, chopped
Fresh thyme	1 sprig
Garlic	5 cloves, peeled and finely chopped
Tomatoes	2
Capers	2 Tbsp
Pickled green olives	15
Vegetable oil	1/2 cup
Onion	1, peeled and finely chopped
Tomato puree	1 can (170 g)
Clear wine or chicken stock	1/2 cup
Water	3/4 cup

Method:

- Season the chicken with lime juice, ground black pepper, salt, spring onions, parsley, fresh thyme and garlic for 30 minutes. Refrigerate.
- Blend the tomatoes, capers and olives into a fine paste. Set aside.
- In a pot, heat the vegetable oil and fry the onion until golden brown. Remove the chicken from the marinade and add in. Cook until chicken changes colour. Add the marinade and stir in the tomato-caper-olive paste and a little water and cook for 20 minutes. Add the tomato puree, clear wine or chicken stock and 3/4 cup water. Stir well, cover and leave to simmer for 45 minutes until gravy thickens.
- Serve hot with rice or pasta.

CHEF'S NOTE: *Use the meat of an older chicken for this recipe, as the cooking process is long and slow. If the meat of a young chicken is used, the dish will not be as tasty and the meat will also break up more easily.*

Bombas de Camarones y Papas
(Prawns and Potato Balls)

These delicious prawn (shrimp) and potato balls can be eaten as a side dish or as a snack at afternoon tea parties. It can be prepared beforehand and stored in the refrigerator overnight. I got this recipe is from Ivan, a Puerto Rican, who was in college with me in San Francisco. The recipe belonged to his grandmother who lived in the Dominican Republic. The Spanish influence is very obvious in this recipe, with the use of potatoes and prawns, which are often served as tapas in Spain.

Ingredients:

Potatoes	500 g, peeled and quartered
Prawns (shrimps)	500 g, shelled and deveined
Butter	3 Tbsp
Cheddar cheese	50 g, grated
Egg yolks	2
Parsley leaves	1 sprig, finely chopped
Salt and ground white pepper to taste	
Onion	1, peeled, diced and stir-fried until soft
Plain (all-purpose) flour	75 g
Egg	1, beaten
Breadcrumbs	100 g
Cooking oil for frying	

Method:
- In a pot, boil the potatoes until soft. Drain and mash the potatoes until smooth.
- Mix the mashed potato with prawns, butter, cheese, egg yolks, parsley, salt, ground white pepper and fried onion.
- Shape the mixture into small balls and dust in plain flour. Dip the balls in the beaten egg and coat with breadcrumbs.
- Fry the balls in a little cooking oil over medium heat until golden brown. Serve with chilli or tomato sauce.

Meat Pies

This meat pie recipe is from Jamaica. I was told that the Indians and Africans who lived on this island long ago were very good money managers. They would keep any leftover food, mince it and mix it with different spices and cook it for another meal. Sometimes, they would also add in garden vegetables, such as young bananas, into the minced food. As a result, a new pie filling was created.

Ingredients:

Pastry:

Plain (all-purpose) flour	300 g, sifted
Salt	1/4 tsp
Vegetable shortening	60 g
Margarine	60 g
Water	1/3 cup

Filling:

Margarine	60 g
Onion	1, peeled and diced
Green chilli	1, finely sliced
Minced meat	300 g
Curry powder	1 1/2 tsp
Ground white pepper to taste	
Fresh thyme	1/2 tsp
Breadcrumbs	30 g
Chicken or beef stock	1/4 cup
Egg	1, beaten

Method:

- Preheat the oven to 200°C.
- Combine the plain flour and salt. Rub in the margarine and vegetable shortening until the mixture resembles breadcrumbs. Pour in the water and knead for a short while until well combined. Cover the dough with a wet cloth and refrigerate.
- In a pan, heat the margarine and sauté the onion and green chilli until soft. Add the minced meat, curry powder, ground white pepper and fresh thyme. Stir-fry the mixture for 10 minutes. Add breadcrumbs and chicken stock and cook until the filling is moist, not wet.
- Roll out the dough and shape into rounds approximately 0.5 cm thick and 12-cm wide. Place a spoonful of filling in the centre of the round and brush some beaten egg around the edges. Fold the round and seal the edges by pressing it down with a fork. Brush some beaten egg over the pie and bake in the oven for 30–35 minutes or until golden brown. Serve hot.

american

Roast Turkey

Making Roast Turkey is not as difficult as most people think it is. Use this recipe to delight your family and friends.

Ingredients:

| Turkey | 1 (10–14 kg) |

Stuffing:

Bread, white or wholemeal	6 cups, cubed and baked till golden brown
Roasted nuts (chestnuts/walnuts)	375 g, finely chopped
Pistachios	30 g, peeled and finely chopped
Raisins (sultanas)	40 g, soaked, drained and dried
Butter	115 g
Onions	2, peeled and finely chopped
Coriander leaves (cilantro)	4 sprigs, thinly chopped
Fresh thyme	1½ tsp
Dried sage leaves	2 tsp (or ground sage 1 tsp)
Green apples	2, cut into medium-sized pieces
Salt and ground white pepper to taste	

Gravy:

Turkey stock	4 cups
Clear dry wine (optional)	1 cup
Butter	60 g
Plain (all-purpose) flour	6 Tbsp, sifted
Salt and ground white pepper to taste	

Method:

For the gravy:

- To prepare the turkey stock, boil the giblet. Add 1 cup of this stock to the juice in roasting pan and stir well. Sieve the juice and add to the remaining stock.
- In a pan, heat the butter and fry the plain flour until golden brown. Add the stock and stir immediately to avoid curdling. Bring to the boil until the mixture thickens. Add salt and white pepper to taste. Serve hot in a separate bowl with the Roast Turkey.

Method:

For the turkey:

- Preheat the oven to 220°C.
- In a large bowl, mix together the baked bread cubes, nuts, pistachios and raisins.
- Melt the butter in a saucepan. Sauté the onions, coriander leaves, thyme and sage until soft. Keep aside.
- Combine the apples and bread-nuts-raisin mixture in the large bowl. Sprinkle salt and ground white pepper to taste. Toss well.
- In a roasting pan, rub salt on the inside and outside of the turkey. Pack a little stuffing in the neck of the turkey. Wrap the lower portion of the neck and secure the edges with toothpicks. Pack the stuffing into the turkey and seal the opening with a string. Turn the turkey so that the breast faces upwards. Season the whole turkey with butter-and-herbs mixture. Keep aside the remaining stuffing.
- Roast in the oven at 220°C for the first 25 minutes then reduce the temperature to 180°C. Baste the turkey with the its juice in the roasting pan. Leave it to roast for 1½–1¾ hours until the juice from the turkey looks clear when the meat is pierced with a skewer. Remove the turkey and wrap in aluminium foil. Keep the juice in the pan.
- Stir 2 tablespoons butter into the remaining stuffing and roast at 200°C for 30 minutes or until golden brown.
- Serve turkey with remaining stuffing and the gravy.

Pumpkin Pie

This is one of the easiest and most suitable desserts for Thanksgiving Day. Whenever I am in San Francisco to celebrate Thanksgiving, I will always prepare this pie. I prefer using American pumpkins for this pie because of its rich colour and taste.

Ingredients:

Pie crust:

Plain (all-purpose) flour	225 g, sifted
Salt	3/4 tsp
Vegetable shortening	150 g
Iced water	3 Tbsp

Pumpkin Custard:

Eggs	2
Evaporated milk	1 1/2 cups
Milk	1/2 cup
Ground allspice	1 tsp
Ground cinnamon	1/2 tsp
Ground ginger	1/2 tsp
Castor sugar	180 g
Honey	1/4 cup
Salt	1/2 tsp
Pumpkin	300 g, cooked and mashed

Method:

For the crust:
- Preheat the oven to 175°C.
- Rub together the plain flour, salt and vegetable shortening until the mixture resembles breadcrumbs. Add iced water to mixture to form a dough.
- Roll out the dough into a sheet 0.5-cm thick and use it to line a 25-cm wide pie mould. Prick the base to flatten the dough. Refrigerate dough for 1 hour.
- When the dough is chilled, line the base with aluminium foil and fill with baking beans, green beans or rice. Bake for 15 minutes until the pie shell is almost cooked. Remove from the oven. Take away the aluminium foil and baking beans.

For the custard:
- In a bowl, beat together the eggs, evaporated milk and milk, ground spices, sugar, honey and salt.
- Add the mashed pumpkin and mix until well combined.
- Pour the mixture into the pie shell and re-bake in the oven for 35 minutes.
- Prick the custard with the tip of a knife to test if the pie is cooked. If the tip of the knife comes out clean, the pie is cooked. Cool and serve.

Potato Salad

There are many varieties of potato salads in America. One of the most popular is the German potato salad. It is made without mayonnaise and is prepared with hot bacon fat. Other salads come with a low-fat yoghurt and sour cream dressing or vinaigrette. The secret to making great and tasty salads is in the balancing of the ingredients—put the dressing on the potatoes while they are still hot to preserve the taste; choose potatoes with high carbohydrate content such as Idaho or Russet potatoes.

Ingredients:

Potatoes	4 large, boiled and cut into small cubes
Mayonnaise	$1/2$ cup
Lemon juice	extracted from $1/2$ lemon
Onion	1, peeled and finely sliced
Sweet gherkins	6, finely chopped
Eggs	2, boiled and sliced
Dijon mustard	1 tsp
Parsley leaves	2 sprigs, finely chopped
Sugar	1 tsp
Salt and ground white pepper to taste.	

Method:
- In a large salad bowl, mix together all the ingredients. Refrigerate for a few hours before serving.

Chef's Note: *This Potato Salad is ideal served as a side dish or as a sandwich filling.*

Barbeque Chicken Wings Texas Style

I visited Mexico in the summer of 1988 and immediately fell in love with their architecture and tasty cuisine. Mexican cooking is very much influenced by Spanish, Pueblo Indian and cowboy traditions and culture. Some of the good southern dishes come from East Texas and are mixed with Mexican styles of cooking and ingredients. These dishes are known as Tex-Mex dishes. This Barbeque Chicken Wings Texas-style recipe is from my friend, Gene Behlan, who lives in Santa Fe, New Mexico.

Ingredients:

Chicken wings	500 g

Sauce:

Dry sherry wine (optional)	½ cup
Lemon juice	2 Tbsp
Tomato puree	2 Tbsp
Demerara sugar	2 Tbsp
Garlic	2 cloves, peeled and finely chopped
Ground cumin	2 Tbsp,
Coriander seeds	1 Tbsp, coarsely pounded
Cayenne pepper	1 tsp
Salt	2 tsp

Method:

- Mix together all the ingredients for the sauce in a bowl. Pour the sauce on the chicken wings and leave to marinate for a few hours before grilling (broiling). Serve hot.

Cornmeal Muffins

This recipe makes a moist and tasty cornmeal muffins. I first used this recipe while I was studying at the California Culinary Academy. We baked hundreds of muffins every day at the Grill Room Restaurant and it was usually never enough.

I enjoy serving this muffin with turkey on Christmas Eve. It tastes best when eaten fresh with butter and honey. The early settlers in America learnt to prepare this muffin from the American Indians. The original recipe used only corn, maple syrup and water, without any fat or milk-based ingredients.

Ingredients:

Cornmeal	250 g
Plain (all-purpose) flour	170 g, sifted
Castor sugar	55 g
Salt	1 tsp
Baking powder	³/₄ tsp
Egg yolks	3
Cream	1 cup
Milk	1¹/₄ cups
Butter	150 g, melted
Egg whites	5

Method:

- Preheat the oven to 180°C.
- Combine the cornmeal, plain flour, castor sugar, salt, baking powder, egg yolks, cream, milk and butter. Mix well and leave the batter to set for 10 minutes.
- Beat egg whites until fluffy and gradually pour into the batter.
- Grease a muffin mould with butter before pouring in the batter. Bake for 20 minutes until the muffins are golden brown. Serve hot.

CHEF'S NOTE: *To make savoury muffins, omit the sugar and add sliced onions, chopped green chillies, ground pecan nuts or grated Cheddar cheese to the batter.*

Clam Chowder

Clam chowder is a vegetable and seafood cream soup. Its consistency must be just right—thick though not as thick as stew, but not too thin either. It also has to be very smooth. This soup was traditionally prepared by the wives of French fishermen in America as a thanksgiving meal when their husbands returned from sea.

Ingredients:

Clams	2 kg, thoroughly washed
Butter	75 g
Leek	1 stalk, thinly sliced
Onions	2, peeled and finely chopped
Dried Thyme	1 tsp
Potatoes	4, peeled and cut into small cubes
Fish and prawn stock	2 cups
Milk	1 cup
Bay leaf	1
Cream	1 cup
Ground white pepper	1 tsp
Salt to taste	

Method:
- Steam the clams for 2–3 minutes until they open. Remove the flesh from the shells and set aside. Reserve any juices for the stock.
- Heat the butter in a pot and sauté the leek, onions and thyme until soft. Add potatoes, stock, milk and bay leaf. Leave to simmer until the potatoes are soft. Remove from heat and put into a blender. Blend into a smooth paste. Transfer the paste back into the pot.
- Reheat the pot and add cream, clam flesh, ground white pepper and salt. Leave to simmer. If the soup is too thick, add more milk or water to dilute it to the desired consistency. Serve hot.

Apple Pancake

The Americans love to eat pancakes especially for breakfast. Pancakes make a hearty breakfast and can be served with a variety of toppings. You may even have them for afternoon tea.

Ingredients:

Pancakes:

Plain (all-purpose) flour	75 g, sifted
Baking powder	1 tsp
Eggs	2
Castor sugar	3 tsp
Vanilla essence	1 tsp
Butter	60 g, melted
Warm milk	3/4 cup

Filling:

Butter	2 Tbsp
Sugar	2 Tbsp
Ground cinnamon	1/4 tsp
Green apples	2, peeled and cut into small cubes

Method:

- In a bowl, sift together the plain flour and baking powder. Set aside.
- In another bowl, beat the eggs, sugar and vanilla essence. Pour in the melted butter and warm milk. Pour the mixture into the sifted flour and mix well. Cover the bowl with a wet towel and leave the batter to set for 10 minutes.
- Meanwhile, prepare the filling. Heat the butter and sugar in a pan and stir continuously until the sugar caramelises. Add the ground cinnamon and apples and fry until the apples are soft and golden brown in colour.
- In a non-stick saucepan, melt a little butter and pour in a spoonful of the pancake batter. Add some apples on the top of the pancake and cook over medium heat. Bubbles should start forming in the batter as the pancake cooks. Slowly ease a spatula around the edges of the pancake to lift it from the pan. Flip the pancake over to cook the other side.
- Serve hot with butter, maple syrup or icing (confectioner's) sugar.

Cream of Pumpkin Soup

I serve this dish every year on Thanksgiving Day. Traditionally, the Americans celebrated Thanksgiving with a feast of dishes made using pumpkins and corn. This delicious Pumpkin Soup may be served with turkey or duck.

Ingredients:

Butter	4 Tbsp
Onion	1, peeled and finely chopped
Curry powder	1/2 tsp
Pumpkin	1 medium (about 2 kg), peeled and diced
Chicken stock	4 cups
Cream	2 cups
Parsley leaves	1 Tbsp, finely chopped
Salt and ground white pepper to taste	

Method:
- Heat the butter in a pot and sauté the onion and curry powder for a few minutes. Add the pumpkin and chicken stock. Boil until the pumpkin is soft.
- Pour the mixture into a blender and blend until smooth. Pour the mixture back into the pot. Add cream, parsley leaves, salt and ground white pepper and bring to the boil before turning off the heat.
- Sprinkle some grated nutmeg on the soup before serving, if desired. Serve hot.

Maryland Crabcakes

Maryland is beautiful in the autumn. I love to watch the maple leaves fall and be gently lifted away by the wind. Autumn, however, also reminds me of the vulnerability of our existence. To see the leaves change colour, fall and wither away reminds me of the transience of time. This crabcake recipe from Maryland is really special. Share it with those you treasure. To get the best out of this recipe, always use fresh crabmeat, not the frozen kind.

Ingredients:

Crabs	1 kg, steamed and shelled
Mayonnaise	2 tsp
Onion or shallot	1, peeled and chopped
Egg yolk	1
Plain (all-purpose) flour	1 Tbsp, sifted
Tabasco sauce	1 tsp
Spring onions (scallions)	2, finely chopped
Red chilli	1, cut into small cubes
Lemon juice	extracted from 1/2 lemon
Parsley leaves	1 sprig, finely chopped
Freshly cracked black peppercorns and salt to taste	
Olive oil for frying	

Method:

- In a bowl, combine all the ingredients except the olive oil. Mix well. Shape the mixture into small balls.
- Fry in hot olive oil until golden brown. Drain on absorbent paper.
- Serve with tartar sauce and a slice of lemon.

Chilli Con Carni

Another favourite American dish, Chilli Con Carni is simple to prepare but delicious. It is ideal as a one-dish meal and goes well with crusty bread or white rice. You can even eat it the American way by scooping it up with corn chips!

Ingredients:

Olive oil	3 Tbsp
Garlic	3 cloves, peeled and chopped
Onions	2, peeled and chopped
Carrot	1, peeled and cut into small cubes
Celery	1 stalk, sliced
Minced beef	900 g
Ground cumin	1 Tbsp
Chilli powder	1 tsp
Stewed tomatoes	1 can (225 g)
Beef stock	4 cups
Coriander leaves (cilantro)	2 sprigs, finely chopped
Red kidney beans	1 can (225 g)
Bay leaf	1
Green chillies	2, finely sliced
Salt and ground white pepper to taste	
Sugar	2 tsp

Method:
- Heat the olive oil in a pan and fry the garlic and onions until fragrant. Add the carrot, celery and minced beef. Slowly stir in the ground cumin and chilli powder.
- Add the tomatoes, beef stock, coriander leaves, red kidney beans, bay leaf and green chillies. Leave to simmer for at least half hour until the mixture thickens. Stir in salt, pepper and sugar. Serve hot.

CHEF'S NOTE: *Make this dish even more appetising topped with a dollop of sour cream and a handful of grated cheddar cheese.*

Georgia Pecan Pie

Quick and easy to make, this delicious Georgia Pecan Pie is great as dessert. It is also suitable as a teatime snack.

Ingredients:

Pie shell	1, 22.5-cm wide, pre-baked (refer to Pumpkin Pie recipe on page 182)
Eggs	3
Demerara sugar	170 g
Corn syrup	½ cup
Unsalted butter	170 g, melted and chilled
Soft molasses	2 Tbsp
Vanilla essence	1 tsp
Roasted pecan nuts	250 g, chopped

Method:

- Preheat the oven to 180°C.
- In a bowl, beat together the eggs, demerara sugar, corn syrup, melted butter, molasses and vanilla essence. Mix in the pecan nuts.
- Pour the filling into the pastry crust. Bake for about 40 minutes.
- Decorate with icing sugar and pecans. Serve with whipped cream.

Allspice
The dried dark brown berries of the pimiento tree, allspice can be purchased whole or ground. It tastes like a combination of cinnamon, nutmeg and cloves.

Amaretto
This liquor has a flavour like almonds.

Aubergines (Eggplants)
Also known as brinjals, this vegetable comes in two varieties — egg-shape and long. They are either white or deep purple. The purple variety has a thicker skin, but there is no difference in flavour.

Bay Leaf
There are two basic varieties of bay leaf — the Indonesian bay leaf (*daun salam*) and the bay laurel leaf commonly found in Western countries. In Asian cooking, the Indonesian bay leaf is used. It is available fresh or dried and is used to flavour meats. The Indonesian bay leaf must be fried or cooked for a while for its flavour to be released. Bay laurel leaf is commonly used in Mediterranean cooking to flavour sauces, stews and grilled meats.

Candlenut
Similar in texture and taste to the macadamia, the candlenut is used as a thickening agent in Asian cooking.

Caper
The flower bud of a bush found in the Mediterranean and in Asia, it is sun-dried and pickled in vinegar or brine. It is sometimes also salted. It has a pungent flavour and is used in sauces and as a garnish.

Cayenne Pepper
A powder made from ground hot peppers.

Chervil
An aromatic herb of the parsley family, chervil is used in soups and salads.

Cinnamon
Sold as sticks or ground into powder, this aromatic spice is derived from the inner bark of the cinnamon tree. It is one of the spices in five spice powder.

Cloves
Resembling a small nail, this deep brown spice is the dried flower bud of the clove tree. It is sold whole or ground and can be used to flavour both sweet and savoury dishes.

Coriander (Cilantro)
Also known as Chinese parsley, coriander leaves have a strong flavour and are used for flavouring and garnishing food. It should not be used as a substitute for English parsley except for garnishing. Coriander leaves are commonly used in Indian, Mexican, Caribbean and Asian cuisine.

Corn Syrup
A thick sweet syrup that comes in a light and dark form. The dark corn syrup has a stronger flavour.

Cornmeal
Cornmeal is made from dried corn kernels ground into a fine, medium or coarse texture. It is available in yellow, white or blue, depending on the type of corn used.

Cornstarch
Also known as corn flour, cornstarch is used as a thickening agent in sauces, soups and stews. The flour is generally dissolved in a small amount of water to form a thin paste before stirring into a hot mixture. Sauces thickened with cornstarch will thin if overcooked or over stirred. Cornstarch is sometimes added to flour in European cookie and cake recipes to make the product more compact and give it a finer texture.

Couscous
A North African dish made from semolina. Precooked couscous is available in supermarkets.

Cumin
Cumin is used in Middle Eastern, Asian and Mediterranean cooking. This aromatic spice has a nutty flavour and is available whole or ground. It is popularly used to flavour curries, stews and Indian yoghurt drinks (lassi).

Desiccated Coconut
Desiccated coconut is available in granular form or strips. It is usually used as a filler for sweets or as a topping for cakes and pastries.

Dill
Dill is available fresh or dried, though the fresh herb has a stronger, more distinctive flavour. Fresh dill loses its flavour through heating and should be added only at the last stages of cooking.

Fennel
This bulb vegetable is white or pale green in colour. It grows in temperate climates and is sold in major super-markets. The root ends and stalks are trimmed before use.

Fenugreek
Fenugreek seeds come whole or ground and are known for their slightly bitter and caramel-like taste. It is used to flavour curry powders, spice blends and teas.

Fish Sauce
Fish sauce or *nam pla* is a pungent but essential ingredient in Thai cooking. It is made from salted fermented fish. Quality fish sauce is clear and brownish in colour.

Coriander leaves

Turmeric

Tarragon

Thymes

Sage

Marjoram

Courgette
(Zucchini)

Kaffir lime leaves

Aubergine
(Eggplant)

Oregano

Kalamansi

Rosemary

Mints

Lemon
grass

Dill

Galangal
Galangal has a hot, peppery flavour and is used mainly as a seasoning. This rhizome can be used as a substitute for ginger and is particularly popular in Thai cooking.

Ghee
Originating from India, ghee is a clarified butter with a nutty, caramel-like flavour and aroma. It used to be made from buffalo milk, but today, it is also made from unsalted butter. Ghee is also commercially made in Holland and Australia.

Gherkins
Gherkins are made from the young fruit of small, dark green cucumbers. They are pickled and sold in jars.

Gruyere cheese
A Swiss cheese with a rich, sweet and nutty flavour. It can be eaten straight from the pack or cooked.

Kaffir Lime
The kaffir lime is dark green in colour and has a knobbly and wrinkled rind. As it ages, the rind turns a lighter yellow green. The fragrant leaves and rind of the kaffir lime are used in Thai and other Southeast Asian cuisine.

Kalamansi
The juice of this small, round, green citrus fruit is very sour. It adds a tangy flavour to dishes and drinks.

Lemon Grass
This long and thin herb has a lemon scent and is available fresh or dried in Asian markets. The whole stem can be added to curries, stews and sauces, but it can also be ground with other ingredients to form a paste.

Marjoram
The most common form of this herb is the sweet marjoram or simply marjoram. Its oval-shaped leaves give off a mild oregano-like flavour. There is also wild marjoram and pot marjoram. Marjoram is available fresh or dried and is used to flavour meat (especially lamb and veal) and vegetable dishes.

Oregano
Oregano is also known as wild marjoram, but it is not as sweet and has a more pungent flavour and aroma. Oregano goes well with tomato-based dishes such as pasta and pizzas.

Paprika
A powder made from dried sweet red peppers, paprika is used both as a seasoning and a garnish.

Phyllo pastry
Phyllo (or filo) pastry is a paper thin pastry that is used in the preparation of sweet or savoury dishes. It can be found packaged fresh in Greek markets or frozen in supermarkets. When opened, the sheets dry out quickly and will become brittle and useless. Remove what you need and keep moist under a damp kitchen towel. Rewrap the rest and refreeze.

Pickled Anchovies
These anchovies are large fillets pickled in spiced vinegar. They taste sweet and are a speciality in Spain.

Red Wine Vinegar
Red wine vinegar is a pungent vinegar made from red wine.

Rose Water
Rose water can be purchased in delicatessens. It has a sweet aroma and is used to flavour Greek pastries, puddings, and cakes.

Rosemary
Rosemary is an aromatic herb with blue-green needle-shaped leaves. The leaves are used fresh or dried to flavour salads, soups, vegetables, meats, stuffing and dressings.

Saffron
Saffron is the world's most expensive spice. The saffron strands are the dried stigmas of the saffron flower and they are used to tint and flavour foods. Because of its strong colour and taste, it can be used sparingly. Saffron is also sold in powdered form, but the flavour is easily lost. It is a principle ingredient in Italian risotto and Spanish paella.

Sage
Sage has a slightly bitter flavour and is available fresh or dried. It is used to flavour soups, vegetables and poultry and is also commonly used in stuffing.

Shrimp Paste
Used in Asian cooking, shrimp paste is available in cake form and may be soft and greyish pink in colour or firm and dark brown in colour. It has a pungent odour and may be used sparingly to flavour rice and sauces.

Tahini
A thick paste made from ground sesame seeds, tahini is used in many Middle Eastern cuisines such as hummus and baba ghanoush.

Tamarind
The seed pod of the tamarind fruit is dried and the resulting pulp is black, sticky and sour. It must be reconstituted in hot water and squeezed to extract its sour flavour. Tamarind is used to flavour meat and fish curries.

Tamarind pulp

Dried
shrimp paste

Couscous

Pickled
anchovy

Capers

Parmesan cheese

Fenugreek

Gerkhins

Saffron
strands

Tahini

Tarragon
A herb that is available both fresh and dried, tarragon adds a distinctive anise-like flavour to food. It is commonly used in French cooking.

Thai Basil Leaves (Bai Horapa)
Thai basil is used in hot and sour Thai soups (*tom yam*) or curries. As it loses its flavour if cooked too long, it should be added only at the last stage of cooking.

Thyme
A savoury herb with a slightly bitter taste, thyme is used to flavour a variety of dishes, from vegetables and meat to soups and cream sauces. It is commonly used in French cuisine.

Turmeric
This yellow coloured rhizome is related to ginger and is used in many dishes in India. Grated turmeric is also added to Thai curries. The fresh root has an aromatic and spicy fragrance, which can be lost by drying. Turmeric is available fresh or ground.

Courgettes (Zucchinis)
This long-shaped squash varies in colour from dark green to light green. It may sometimes have markings on its skin. When choosing courgettes, select small, vibrant coloured ones. These tend to be younger and more tender. Courgettes can be steamed, fried, grilled or baked.

Quantities for this book are given in Metric and American (spoon and cup) measures. Standard spoon and cup measurements used are: 1 tsp = 5 ml, 1 dsp = 10 ml, 1 Tbsp = 15 ml, 1 cup = 250 ml.

All measures are level unless otherwise stated.

LIQUID AND VOLUME MEASURES

Metric	Imperial	American
5 ml	1/6 fl oz	1 tsp
10 ml	1/3 fl oz	1 dsp
15 ml	1/2 fl oz	1 Tbsp
60 ml	2 fl oz	1/4 cup (4 Tbsp)
85 ml	2 1/2 fl oz	1/3 cup
90 ml	3 fl oz	3/8 cup (6 Tbsp)
125 ml	4 fl oz	1/2 cup
180 ml	6 fl oz	3/4 cup
250 ml	8 fl oz	1 cup
300 ml	10 fl oz (1/2 pint)	1 1/4 cups
375 ml	12 fl oz	1 1/2 cups
435 ml	14 fl oz	1 3/4 cups
500 ml	16 fl oz	2 cups
625 ml	20 fl oz (1 pint)	2 3/4 cups
750 ml	24 fl oz (1 3/5 pints)	3 cups
1 litre	32 fl oz (1 3/5 pints)	4 cups
1.25 litres	40 fl oz (2 pints)	5 cups
1.5 litres	48 fl oz (2 2/5 pints)	6 cups
2.5 litres	80 fl oz (4 pints)	10 cups

DRY MEASURES

Metric	Imperial
30 g	1 ounce
45 g	1 1/2 ounces
55 g	2 ounces
70 g	2 1/2 ounces
85 g	3 ounces
100 g	3 1/2 ounces
110 g	4 ounces
125 g	4 1/2 ounces
140 g	5 ounces
280 g	10 ounces
450 g	16 ounces (1 pound)
500 g	1 pound, 1 1/2 ounces
700 g	1 1/2 pounds
800 g	1 3/4 pounds
1 kg	2 pounds, 3 ounces
1.5 kg	3 pounds, 4 1/2 ounces
2 kg	4 pounds, 6 ounces

OVEN TEMPERATURE

	°C	°F	Gas Regulo
Very slow	120	250	1
Slow	150	300	2
Moderately slow	160	325	3
Moderate	180	350	4
Moderately hot	190/200	370/400	5/6
Hot	210/220	410/440	6/7
Very hot	230	450	8
Super hot	250/290	475/550	9/10

LENGTH

Metric	Imperial
0.5 cm	1/4 inch
1 cm	1/2 inch
1.5 cm	3/4 inch
2.5 cm	1 inch